T0323900

"Clear, engaging and insightful, there is no better introduction to the past, present and future of phenomenological philosophy than this new edition of Zahavi's book."

– Dave Ward, University of Edinburgh, UK

"Nuanced, problem-driven, and accessible, this is simply the best introduction to phenomenology. Lucidly written, it presents clear explanations of key concepts and theories while covering the breadth of the phenomenological tradition. The revised edition now also provides an introduction to Critical Phenomenology, likely the most-discussed trend in phenomenology today."

– Tobias Keiling, University of Warwick, UK

Praise for the previous edition:

"For the one seeking a way into phenomenological thinking today, or a way to help others find one, it has not been obvious, in the English context, what resource should serve as the best point of entry. The first great merit of Dan Zahavi's book, *Phenomenology: The Basics*, is to change this calculus for good. Offering English readers an entry point into phenomenology that is accessible, lucid, and engaging, presents key concepts and insights faithfully (but not ploddingly), along with their pertinence in multiple fields of contemporary research, and doing this without obvious error or negligence, is no small achievement."

– Karl Hefty, Reading Religion

"A lucid and authoritative introduction to phenomenology including its practical applications in sociology and psychology from one of the world's leading phenomenologists."

– Dermot Moran, Boston College, USA

"Zahavi's *Phenomenology: The Basics* will guide several generations of philosophers and scientists in the study of consciousness, embodiment, communality and normality."

– Sara Heinämaa, University of Jyväskylä, Finland

PHENOMENOLOGY

THE BASICS

Phenomenology: The Basics is a concise and engaging introduction to one of the important philosophical movements of the twentieth century and to a subject that continues to grow and diversify. Yet it is also a challenging subject, the elements of which can be hard to grasp.

This lucid book provides an introduction to the core ideas of phenomenology and to the arguments of its principal thinkers, including Husserl, Heidegger, and Merleau-Ponty. Written by a leading expert in the field, Dan Zahavi examines and explains key questions such as:

- What is a phenomenological analysis?
- What are the methodological foundations of phenomenology?
- What does phenomenology have to say about intentionality, embodiment, intersubjectivity, and the lifeworld?
- How do ideas from classic phenomenology relate to ongoing debates in qualitative research and the cognitive sciences?

This second edition has been thoroughly revised and expanded. It contains a new chapter on critical phenomenology and updated discussions of the application of phenomenology in psychiatry, psychology, and qualitative research.

Including a glossary of key terms and suggestions for further reading, *Phenomenology: The Basics* is a superb starting point for anyone seeking a concise and accessible introduction to this rich and fascinating subject.

Dan Zahavi is Professor of Philosophy at the University of Copenhagen, Denmark, and Director of the Center for Subjectivity Research in Copenhagen. His book *The Phenomenological Mind* (third edition, 2021), coauthored with Shaun Gallagher, is also available from Routledge.

THE BASICS

The Basics is a highly successful series of accessible guidebooks which provide an overview of the fundamental principles of a subject area in a jargon-free and undaunting format.

Intended for students approaching a subject for the first time, the books both introduce the essentials of a subject and provide an ideal springboard for further study. With over 50 titles spanning subjects from Artificial Intelligence to Women's Studies, *The Basics* are an ideal starting point for students seeking to understand a subject area.

Each text comes with recommendations for further study and gradually introduces the complexities and nuances within a subject.

ATHEISM
GRAHAM OPPY

PERCEPTION
BENCE NANAY

EMOTION
MICHAEL BRADY

PHILOSOPHY OF TIME
GRAEME FORBES

PHILOSOPHY OF MIND
AMY KIND

CAUSATION
STUART GLENNAN

METAPHYSICS (SECOND EDITION)
MICHAEL REA

PHILOSOPHY OF LANGUAGE
ETHAN NOWAK

FREE WILL (SECOND EDITION)
MEGHAN GRIFFITH

STOIC ETHICS
CHRISTOPHER GILL AND BRITTANY POLAT

CRITICAL THINKING (SECOND EDITION)
STUART HANSCOMB

POLITICAL PHILOSOPHY
BAS VAN DER VOSSEN

GLOBAL DEVELOPMENT
DANIEL HAMMETT

INTERVIEWING
MARK HOLTON

FOOD ETHICS (SECOND EDITION)
RONALD SANDLER

PHENOMENOLOGY (SECOND EDITION)
DAN ZAHAVI

Other titles in the series can be found at: https://www.routledge.com/The-Basics/book-series/B

PHENOMENOLOGY

THE BASICS

SECOND EDITION

Dan Zahavi

Routledge
Taylor & Francis Group

LONDON AND NEW YORK

Designed cover image: 'Abstract watercolour background with colorful circles on black', by Olga_Z. Courtesy of Getty Images

Second edition published 2025
by Routledge
4 Park Square, Milton Park, Abingdon, Oxon OX14 4RN

and by Routledge
605 Third Avenue, New York, NY 10158

Routledge is an imprint of the Taylor & Francis Group, an informa business

First edition published by Routledge 2018

British Library Cataloguing-in-Publication Data
A catalogue record for this book is available from the British Library

ISBN: 978-1-032-39638-5 (hbk)
ISBN: 978-1-032-39637-8 (pbk)
ISBN: 978-1-003-35068-2 (ebk)

DOI: 10.4324/9781003350682

Typeset in Bembo and Scala Sans
by Apex CoVantage, LLC

For Eliyahu

CONTENTS

PREFACE TO THE SECOND EDITION

Back in 2003, I published a short introduction to phenomenology in Danish. In the years that followed, the book was translated into German (2007), Icelandic (2008), and Japanese (2015). In 2016, I contacted Routledge and asked whether they might be interested in publishing an English translation. We quickly reached an agreement, but when I started translating the text from Danish, I came to realize that there were many ways in which the original text from 2003 could be improved upon. In the end, I decided to rework and rewrite the entire text completely. The result became a much longer and, I believe, far better book.

The first edition was published in 2019. I am grateful to Routledge for encouraging me to work on a revised and expanded second edition. The changes to the first eight chapters are fairly modest. They include some minor tweaks and stylistic improvements and in the case of Chapter 7 some condensations, but the introduction is expanded, Chapter 9 is new, and chapters 10–12 have been rewritten.

I dedicate this second edition to the memory of my father Eliyahu Zahavi, a self-taught journalist, who always supported my own education.

INTRODUCTION

Phenomenology counts as one of the dominant traditions in 20th-century philosophy. Edmund Husserl was its founder, but other influential proponents were Max Scheler, Martin Heidegger, Edith Stein, Jean-Paul Sartre, Maurice Merleau-Ponty, and Emmanuel Levinas. One reason for its influence is that almost all subsequent theory formations in German and French philosophy can be understood as either extensions of or reactions to phenomenology. A proper grasp of phenomenology is, consequently, important not only for its own sake, but also because it remains a *sine qua non* for an understanding of subsequent developments in philosophy in the 20th and 21st centuries.

Over the years, phenomenology has made major contributions to many areas of philosophy and offered groundbreaking analyses of topics such as intentionality, perception, embodiment, emotions, self-consciousness, intersubjectivity, temporality, historicity, and truth. It has delivered a targeted criticism of reductionism, objectivism, and scientism, and argued at length for a rehabilitation of the lifeworld. By presenting a detailed account of human existence, where the subject is understood as an embodied and socially and culturally embedded being-in-the-world, phenomenology has provided crucial inputs to a whole range of empirical disciplines,

DOI: 10.4324/9781003350682-1

including psychiatry, sociology, psychology, anthropology, nursing studies, and the cognitive sciences.

Even though many of the by-now classical works in phenomenology were written in the first half of the 20th century, phenomenology continues to be a source of inspiration and has in recent years been the subject of renewed interest. Indeed, it would not be an exaggeration to claim that phenomenology is currently undergoing something of a renaissance.

Although phenomenology has, in many ways, developed as a heterogeneous movement with many branches; although all post-Husserlian phenomenologists have distanced themselves from various aspects of Husserl's original programme; and although it would be an exaggeration to claim that phenomenology is a philosophical system with a clearly delineated body of doctrines, one should not overlook the overarching philosophical concerns and common themes that have united and continue to unite its proponents.

Given that it will be impossible to do justice to all the phenomenologists in an introduction like the present, I will primarily draw on the work of Husserl, (the early) Heidegger, and Merleau-Ponty – three thinkers whose decisive influence on the development of phenomenology is undeniable. Whereas many introductory books on phenomenology contain separate chapters on these thinkers, I will proceed differently. Rather than articulating and highlighting their differences – differences that, in my view, have often been overstated due to a fundamental misinterpretation of Husserl's founding ideas – my emphasis will instead primarily be on their commonalities.

In the first part of the book, I will focus on the very conception of philosophy found in phenomenology. I will discuss the question of method, the focus on the first-person perspective, the analysis of the lifeworld, and also briefly describe how the tradition has developed.

In the second part of the book, I will put the more methodological considerations to the side, and instead offer some detailed examples of concrete phenomenological analyses. I will first consider phenomenological explorations of spatiality and embodiment, and then turn to analyses of intersubjectivity and community. The final chapter of part two, which to some extent can be seen as a transitional chapter to the final part, will discuss the recent emergence of what has become known as critical phenomenology and offer some examples of how a phenomenological perspective that is more attuned to social and political issues approaches the phenomenon of embodiment.

The third part of the book will demonstrate how phenomenology has been applied outside of philosophy. I will discuss both classical contributions from the fields of psychology, psychiatry, and sociology, and more recent discussions within qualitative research and the cognitive sciences.

My main ambition in writing this book has been to present rather than defend phenomenology. In short, the aim has been to expound a number of distinctive phenomenological ideas in as accessible a way as possible, and not to defend these ideas against the various criticisms they have been subjected to. Readers interested in a more systematic defence of phenomenology or in a more extensive scholarly engagement with the research literature are better served by looking elsewhere.[1]

DRAMATIS PERSONAE

Edmund Husserl (1859–1938)

Husserl came to philosophy at a relatively late age. Born in Proßnitz, Moravia (then part of the Austrian Empire), he studied physics, mathematics, astronomy, and philosophy in Leipzig, Berlin, and Vienna. He obtained his doctoral dissertation in mathematics in 1883, and it was only during the following years that he became seriously interested in philosophy, partially as a result of attending lectures by the psychologist and philosopher Franz Brentano. Husserl's first major work, *Logical Investigations*, was published in 1900–1901, and it was on the basis of this work that Husserl obtained a position at the university in Göttingen, where he taught from 1901 to 1916. His next major work, *Ideas Pertaining to a Pure Phenomenology and to a Phenomenological Philosophy I*, was published in 1913. In 1916, Husserl moved to Freiburg, where he took over the chair in philosophy from the neo-Kantian Heinrich Rickert. In the following years, both Edith Stein and Martin Heidegger worked as his assistants. When Husserl retired in 1928, he was succeeded by Heidegger. Shortly after his retirement, Husserl was invited to Paris to give a series of lectures meant to introduce a French audience to the basic ideas of phenomenology. These lectures were later translated into French by Emmanuel Levinas and Gabrielle Peiffer and published as *Cartesian Meditations* in 1931. During the thirties, Husserl came to suffer under the German National Socialist Regime. Barred from any kind of official academic activity due to his Jewish ancestry, Husserl in turn lost his right to teach, to publish, and eventually also to his German citizenship. Deeply affected by this development, Husserl nevertheless continued his work, insisting even more passionately on the relevance of philosophy at a time when Europe was descending into irrationalism. In 1935, Husserl was invited to give lectures in Vienna and Prague, and these lectures constituted the foundation for his last work, *The Crisis of European Sciences and Transcendental Phenomenology: An Introduction to Phenomenological Philosophy* (1936). Shortly after Husserl's death on April 27, 1938, a young Franciscan Herman Leo van Breda succeeded in smuggling Husserl's many research manuscripts out of Germany and into safety in a monastery in Belgium. Before the start of the Second World War, the Husserl Archives were established in Leuven, where the original manuscripts are still to be found.

Max Scheler (1874–1928)

Max Scheler was brought up in an orthodox Jewish household in Munich. He studied medicine, philosophy, and psychology in Munich, Berlin, and Jena, and obtained his doctorate from the latter university in 1897. In 1901, Scheler met Husserl for the first time. It was a meeting that would prove quite decisive for Scheler. As he was subsequently to write, "I owe the methodological consciousness of the unity and sense of the phenomenological attitude to the work of Husserl", while then continuing, "I take full responsibility for the manner in which I understand and execute this attitude".[2] Scheler was notorious for his rather tumultuous private life. In 1899, Scheler converted to Catholicism and married Amélie von Dewitz-Krebs, an unhappy marriage that quickly fell apart, allegedly because of Scheler's many love affairs. Ongoing marital problems led to a number of public scandals that eventually saw Scheler lose his teaching position and forced him to earn his income as a lecturer, essayist, and publicist in the years 1910–1919. By 1913, Scheler had, however, managed to gain such a standing in phenomenological circles that he was asked by Husserl to become co-editor of the newly established *Jahrbuch für Philosophie und Phänomenologische Forschung* (*Yearbook for Philosophy and Phenomenological Research*). During this period, Scheler also published some of his most influential works, including *Phenomenology and Theory of the Feeling of Sympathy and of Love and Hate* (later republished in an extended version under the better-known title of *On the Nature of Sympathy*) and *Formalism in Ethics and Non-Formal Ethics of Value*. Scheler's reputation continued to grow and by the end of the First World War, he was considered one of the most influential Catholic thinkers in Germany. Shortly after taking up a position as professor of philosophy in Cologne in 1919, however, Scheler publicly distanced himself from the Catholic faith. This not only alienated him from his erstwhile supporters in Cologne, but also from many of his phenomenological colleagues who, due to his influence, had converted to Catholicism. In 1928, Scheler was offered the chair in philosophy and sociology at the University of Frankfurt. He accepted the position, but his deteriorating health – most likely due to his habit of smoking 60–80 cigarettes per day – culminated in a series of heart attacks, and on May 19, 1928, he died of heart failure.

Martin Heidegger (1889–1976)

Heidegger started out studying Catholic theology and medieval philosophy in Freiburg, but in 1911 decided to concentrate on philosophy. In 1913 he defended his dissertation, and two years later his habilitation entitled *Duns Scotus' Theory of the Categories and of Meaning*. The latter work was submitted to Rickert, the philosopher whose successor was Husserl. Heidegger worked as Husserl's assistant from 1918 until 1923, when he became extraordinary professor at the university in Marburg. In 1927, Heidegger's main opus *Being and Time* was published, and in 1928 he took over Husserl's chair in Freiburg. In 1929, Heidegger gave his famous inaugural lecture *What is Metaphysics?* After Hitler's assumption of power, Heidegger was elected rector of Freiburg University, and became a member of the Nazi Party. Less than a year later, however, he stepped down from his rectorship and slowly withdrew from university politics. As the 2014 publication of his so-called *Black Notebooks*, a kind of philosophical diary, demonstrates, Heidegger's flirtation with Nazism was, however, neither short-lived nor superficial. Until 1944, Heidegger gave regular lectures, but after the end of the war he was prohibited from teaching because of his political sympathies, and in 1946 he was deprived of his professorship. Heidegger was reinstated as professor emeritus in 1949, and from then, and until shortly before his death, he lectured extensively, and it was during this period that central works such as *Language* (1950), *Building Dwelling Thinking* (1951), and *The Question Concerning Technology* (1953) were written.

Edith Stein (1891–1942)

Stein was born into a Jewish family in Breslau, Prussia (now Wroclaw, Poland). She initially studied psychology at the University of Breslau, but one of her professors introduced her to Husserl's *Logical Investigations*, a work she found so interesting that she in 1913 decided to transfer to Göttingen in order to study with Husserl. Stein became an active member of the Göttingen Philosophical Society, which was composed of a group of young and active phenomenologists (Adolf Reinach, Roman Ingarden, Hedwig Conrad-Martius). Eventually, Husserl accepted Stein as his doctoral student and recommended her to work on empathy. She graduated *summa cum laude* in 1916, and part of the dissertation was subsequently published as *On the Problem of Empathy*. After her graduation, Stein became Husserl's assistant. Her primary work was to edit Husserl's research manuscripts and prepare them for publication. She worked on Husserl's *Ideas II* (eventually published in 1952) and his *Lectures on the Consciousness of Internal time* (published by Heidegger in 1928, with only the slightest acknowledgment of Stein's work). Rather than engaging with Stein's revisions, Husserl tended to produce new texts and in the end this lack of engagement with her work made Stein resign from her position in frustration. At this point, Stein's academic career hit a stumbling block. Because of being both a woman and Jewish she was unable to obtain permission to submit her intended habilitation thesis *Philosophy of Psychology and the*

Humanities despite trying at various universities. For a while Stein then worked as a private tutor, but through conversations with Theodor Conrad and Hedwig Conrad-Martius, she became interested in Thomas Aquinas and Teresa of Ávila and converted to Catholicism. Stein eventually obtained a teaching position at the German Institute for Scientific Pedagogy in Münster, but after the rise to power of the National Socialists, she was dismissed from her job. In October 1933, Stein was admitted to the Discalced Carmelite monastery in Cologne. In 1938, she transferred for safety reasons to a convent in the Netherlands, though that country did not remain a safe haven for long. The condemnation of Nazi racism by the Dutch bishops on July 20, 1942, infuriated the German authorities and led to them arresting baptised Catholics of Jewish origin in Nazi-occupied Netherlands. Stein was imprisoned by the Gestapo, and sent to Auschwitz, where she was murdered in the gas chambers on August 9, 1942. Stein was canonised as a saint by Pope John Paul II in 1998.

Jean-Paul Sartre (1905–1980)

Sartre studied philosophy at École Normale Supérieure, where he met a whole generation of leading French intellectuals, including Simone de Beauvoir, Raymond Aron, Maurice Merleau-Ponty, Simone Weil, Emmanuel Mounier, Jean Hippolyte, and Claude Lévi-Strauss. His relation to his fellow philosopher Beauvoir became legendary. In the period 1931–1945, Sartre taught at high schools in Le Havre, Laon, and Paris. He was introduced to Husserl's and Heidegger's philosophy in the early thirties by Aron and Levinas, and in 1933–1934 went to Berlin to study phenomenology. In the second half of the thirties, Sartre published four books on consciousness: *The Transcendence of the Ego* (1936), which dealt with the structure of self-consciousness, *Imagination* (1936), *The Imaginary* (1940), and *Sketch for Theory of the Emotions* (1939). All four works reveal Sartre's familiarity with Husserl's philosophy. At the outbreak of the Second World War, Sartre was drafted and was taken prisoner by the Germans in 1940. During his captivity, Sartre studied Heidegger's *Being and Time*. After his release in 1941, Sartre became active in the resistance, and in 1943 published his philosophical masterpiece *Being and Nothingness*, which shows Heidegger's increasing influence.

In 1945, Sartre established the literary and political review *Les Temps Moderne* (*Modern Times*), which he edited for many years (in periods jointly with Merleau-Ponty). After the war, Sartre decided to stop teaching in order to devote himself to his literary and editorial work. Sartre is, consequently, one of the very few influential 20th-century philosophers who was not employed at a university. During the post-war period, Sartre's political engagement increased, as did his sympathy for Marxism and his admiration for the Soviet Union, although he never became a member of the Communist party. Sartre's support for the Soviet Union remained intact until the Soviet invasion of Hungary in 1956. In 1960, Sartre published his second main work, *Critique of Dialectical Reason*, which testifies to his political and social engagement. In 1964, Sartre was awarded the Nobel Prize in Literature, but declined it. Sartre remained politically active until late in life. He opposed France's war in Algeria, was active against the Vietnam War along with Bertrand Russell, and was also a vocal supporter of the May 1968 protests in Paris. When Sartre died in April 1980, 50,000 people attended his funeral.

Maurice Merleau-Ponty (1908–1961)

Merleau-Ponty studied philosophy at the prestigious École Normale Supérieure in Paris, where he befriended Simone de Beauvoir and Claude Lévi-Straus. He attended Husserl's lectures in Paris, and although Merleau-Ponty was not fluent in German at the time, the lectures nevertheless made such an impression that Merleau-Ponty began a more detailed study of Husserl's writings. A few years later, in the spring of 1939, he became the first foreign visitor to the newly established Husserl Archives in Leuven, Belgium. The war and the German invasion of Belgium put a temporary stop to the contact between Paris and Leuven, but already in 1942, Merleau-Ponty took the first steps to establish a research centre in Paris, which should contain copies of Husserl's manuscripts. The same year, Merleau-Ponty published his first book, *The Structure of Behavior*. This was followed in 1945 by what is arguably his main work, *Phenomenology of Perception*. In 1949, Merleau-Ponty became professor of child psychology and pedagogy at the Sorbonne, and in 1952 he was elected to the chair of philosophy at the Collège de France, the youngest ever appointed to the position, which he held until his untimely death in May 1961. After the Second World War, Merleau-Ponty became increasingly engaged in politics, and he published a number of books of essays, including *Humanism and Terror* (1947), *Sense and Non-Sense* (1948), and *Adventures of the Dialectic* (1955). In parallel with his political interests, Merleau-Ponty continued teaching, and many of his lectures from the Sorbonne and Collège de France bear witness to his extensive interest in other disciplines, including child psychology, structural linguistics, ethnology, and psychoanalysis. In 1960, *Signs*, another volume consisting of essays, was published, and in 1964 the fragmentary *The Visible and the Invisible*, which many consider Merleau-Ponty's second main work, was published posthumously.

Emmanuel Levinas (1906–1995)

Emmanuel Levinas was born in Kaunas in Lithuania (then part of the Russian Empire). After completing high school, Levinas left for France where he started philosophy studies in Strasbourg. In 1928, he spent time in Freiburg in Germany studying with Husserl and Heidegger. When his doctoral dissertation, *The Theory of Intuition in Husserl's Phenomenology*, was published in 1931, Levinas's reputation as one of the foremost experts on German phenomenology in France was consolidated. By the time of the outbreak of the Second World War, Levinas had become a French citizen, and was drafted into the army. Like Sartre, he was soon captured and spent the rest of the war in German captivity. He was thereby spared the fate of most of his Jewish family who were killed by the Germans. After the war Levinas became the director of the École Normale Israélite Orientale in Paris, and then obtained positions at the University of Poitiers (1961), Nanterre (1967), and from 1973 at the Sorbonne in Paris. Levinas's early post-war works *From Existence to Existents* (1947), *Time and the Other* (1948), and *Discovering Existence with Husserl and Heidegger* (1949) display his indebtedness to both Husserl and Heidegger, but already announce themes that characterise Levinas's own thinking, such as the role of the other and the relation between ethics and ontology. Levinas's work on these latter topics reached its culmination in his two masterpieces, *Totality and Infinity* (1961) and

Otherwise than Being or Beyond Essence (1974). Next to many philosophical books, Levinas also published a series of Talmudic commentaries and essays on Judaism.

NOTES

1 See, for instance, Zahavi, D. (2003). *Husserl's Phenomenology*. Stanford, CA: Stanford University Press; Zahavi, D. (2005). *Subjectivity and Selfhood: Investigating the First-Person Perspective*. Cambridge, MA: MIT Press; Zahavi, D. (2014). *Self and Other: Exploring Subjectivity, Empathy, and Shame*. Oxford: Oxford University Press; Zahavi, D. (2017). *Husserl's Legacy: Phenomenology, Metaphysics, and Transcendental Philosophy*. Oxford: Oxford University Press; Gallagher, S. and Zahavi, D. (2021). *The Phenomenological Mind*. 3rd edn. London: Routledge.
2 Scheler, M. (1973). *Formalism in Ethics and Non-Formal Ethics of Values: A New Attempt Toward a Foundation of an Ethical Personalism*, trans. M.S. Frings and R.L. Funk. Evanston, IL: Northwestern University Press: xi.

SUGGESTIONS FOR FURTHER READING

Dermot Moran, *Introduction to Phenomenology*. London: Routledge, 2000.
Herbert Spiegelberg, *The Phenomenological Movement: A Historical Introduction*. The Hague: Martinus Nijhoff, 1965.

PART I

FOUNDATIONAL ISSUES

The aim of the following six chapters is to offer a basic overview of what phenomenology is all about. What kind of exploration is it engaged in? Is phenomenology primarily or even exclusively focused on the mind or is it equally about the world? What is a phenomenon in the first place, and how do we go about investigating it? What are the different ways in which we can relate to the world? What is the difference between talking about a tree and perceiving it? How does the world of science relate to the world we know from everyday experience? And what does it mean to say that phenomenology is a form of transcendental philosophy? The chapters will present some of the overarching themes and problems of phenomenology, describe its method(s), and outline its development.

DOI: 10.4324/9781003350682-2

FOUNDATIONAL ISSUES

THE PHENOMENA

Strictly speaking, phenomenology means the science or study of phenomena. But what is a phenomenon? And what kind of phenomena do phenomenologists investigate? Are they mainly interested in spectacular phenomena, in truly phenomenal phenomena? In her autobiography, Simone de Beauvoir recounts how Sartre was first introduced to Husserl's phenomenology. They were both visiting a cocktail bar with their friend Raymond Aron, who had just returned from Germany. Aron pointed to the apricot cocktail he had ordered and said to Sartre: "You see, my dear fellow, if you are a phenomenologist, you can talk about this cocktail and make philosophy out of it!"[1] Aron was quite right. Even the everyday experience of simple objects can serve as the point of departure for a phenomenological analysis. Indeed, if philosophy is to avoid the dead end of stale abstractions, it has to reconnect to the richness of everyday life. Importantly, however, phenomenology is interested in *how* rather than merely in *what* we experience. Rather than simply focusing on, say, the weight, rarity, or chemical composition of the object of experience, phenomenology is concerned with the way in which the object shows or displays itself, i.e., in how it appears. There are important differences between the ways in which a physical object, a utensil, a work of art, a melody, a state of affairs, a

DOI: 10.4324/9781003350682-3

number, or other human beings present themselves. Moreover, it is possible for one and the same object to appear in a variety of different ways: From this or that perspective, in strong or faint illumination, as perceived, imagined, wished for, feared, anticipated, or recollected. Briefly stated, phenomenology can be seen as a philosophical analysis of these different types of givenness.

THE ALARM CLOCK

This might all sound very abstract, so let us consider a concrete example. I am on the lookout for a birthday present for a friend of mine and am searching in a vintage shop in central Copenhagen. At some point, I notice an antique alarm clock. How does an alarm clock appear? What kind of phenomenon is it? To start with, we should recognise that there is no simple answer to this question, since an alarm clock can appear in numerous ways. Not only can I see, touch, and hear it, but it can also appear in thought, just as I might see a picture of it or simply use it. To keep matters simple for now, let us just focus on the way the alarm clock appears in the situation in question, namely perceptually. Depending on the illumination (natural sunlight, neon lights, spotlights, etc.), the alarm clock will appear differently. Regardless of the circumstances, however, and even under optimal lighting conditions, I will never be able to see the entire alarm clock, since it will always appear perspectivally. If I look at the alarm clock as it is positioned on the desk in the shop, I might be able to see its top, and two of its sides, but I cannot see its backside or bottom or inside. If I move around the desk, I might be able to see the backside of the alarm clock. If I lift it from the desk, I might be able to inspect its bottom, but regardless of what I do, the alarm clock will continue to appear perspectivally. When new aspects are revealed, former aspects will disappear from view. This might seem like a fairly trivial observation, something so taken for granted in daily life that no further thoughts are required, but in the hands of the phenomenologists, it contains the key to a wealth of insights. Consider first the fact that although we never see the entire alarm clock, we do not doubt or in any way question that there is more to the alarm clock than what appears. It has parts and properties which are not perceptually present. In fact, these absent aspects play a role in our perception, even when absent. Without them, the front of the alarm clock would not appear as a front. Perceptual experience consequently involves an interplay of presence and absence. When we perceive an object, we always experience more than what is intuitively presented. The front that we do see points to other sides of the alarm clock that are momentarily absent, but which can be revealed by further exploration. More generally speaking, what we see is never given in isolation, but is surrounded by and situated in a horizon that affects the meaning of what we see.

This horizon encompasses more than simply the momentarily unseen aspects of the object in question. After all, we never encounter isolated objects, but only objects that are embedded within a larger context. The alarm clock I am looking at is standing on a desk that is located in a particular room, and depending on whether the room in question is a salesroom, an examination hall, or a lawyer's office, the alarm clock will appear in different ways, with different meanings.

My field of consciousness is not exhausted by the alarm clock, even if I am attending to it. The alarm clock might be surrounded by other watches, cups, pens, a couple of books, etc. When focusing on the alarm clock, I do not pay attention to its surroundings. But I am not oblivious to the other utensils, the floor I am standing on, the illumination in the room, etc. I am merely conscious of them as ground, i.e., they are parts of the totality which serve as the background for attending to the alarm clock. And although these objects belong to the background, they can become themes in their own right through a change of attention. Indeed, the possibility of such a thematic change is exactly based on the fact that my theme is situated in a field that is co-given with it, and in which I can mentally (and physically) move around.

To proceed further in our analysis, let us consider for a moment what it means to say that the alarm clock appears perspectivally. When the alarm clock appears perceptually, it always appears at a certain angle and at a certain distance from the perceiver. But what does this tell us about the perceiver? For the alarm clock to appear in the way it does, the perceiver must be located in the same space that is occupied by the alarm clock. But for the perceiver to be spatially located is for the perceiver to be embodied. A truly disembodied perceiver would have no spatial location, or, to put it differently, the alarm clock can only appear the way it does to an embodied perceiver. There is no purely intellectual point of view and there is no view from nowhere, there is only an embodied point of view.

That the body plays a crucial role in perception can also be illustrated in a slightly different manner. Even if we initially are only confronted with a very limited perspective on the object, we rarely remain satisfied with the first glimpse. As Husserl points out, the object beckons us to explore further:

> There is still more to see here, turn me so you can see all my sides, let your gaze run through me, draw closer to me, open me up, divide me up; keep on looking me over again and again, turning me to see all sides. You will get to know me like this, all that I am, all my surface qualities, all my inner sensible qualities.[2]

How do we carry out such an exploration? How do we get to know the alarm clock better? By picking it up by hand and turning it around, or by walking around the desk so that we can observe its backside. But all of this calls for and involves bodily engagement and interaction. We consequently learn that perceptual exploration, rather than being a question of an immobile intake of information, is a bodily activity. We move our eyes, our head, our torso, our arms and hands, and our entire body. This activity, this bodily exploration, this getting to know the alarm clock better by discovering more and more of its aspects, is not instantaneous. It takes time. And time does indeed play a crucial role as well. When first looking at the front of the alarm clock and then moving around to observe its back, the front might gradually disappear from sight, but not from mind. Our familiarity with the alarm clock increases because we are able to retain that which we have seen in the past. When executing a change of perspective and position, we do not first experience the front of the alarm clock and then its side and then its back as if we were viewing three distinct snapshots. If we pick up the alarm clock and turn it around in our hand, we experience how its appearance changes gradually, rather than abruptly. But for the alarm clock to appear in this manner, our stream of consciousness cannot be a series of instantaneous and disconnected perceptions, but must have a particular temporal structure and configuration, must somehow be temporally and experientially unified. In addition, time also plays a different role here. When highlighting the importance of context and horizon, we shouldn't merely think of this in spatial terms, but also in temporal terms. We encounter the present on the basis of the past, and with plans and expectations for the future. Our past experiences are not lost and do not leave us untouched. When noticing the alarm clock, I decided to investigate it further, not only because I knew from past experiences that my friend is a heavy sleeper, but also because of my plans for the future – I intended to present him with a gift.

This brings me to the last point I want to extract from this example. When the alarm clock appears, it appears to me, but it does not appear to me as my private object. Rather, it is very much given to me as a public object, as one that others can also observe and utilise. Which, of course, is also why I would consider buying it in the first place. Even if the alarm clock only presents part of itself to me, others can simultaneously perceive aspects of it that are currently unavailable to me.

APPEARANCE AND REALITY

But what is the relevance of all of this, one might ask. By focusing on how various objects appear, phenomenology only tells us something about the phenomena, i.e., about the apparent nature of objects, about what objects *apparently* are. And surely this must be contrasted with the goal of science, which is to grasp the objects as they truly are.

In much of the philosophical tradition, the phenomenon has indeed been defined as the way the object appears to us, as seen with our eyes (and thought of with our categories), and has been contrasted with the object as it is in itself. The assumption has then been that if one wishes to discover and determine what the object really is like, then one has to go beyond the merely phenomenal. Had it been this concept of the phenomenon that phenomenology was employing, phenomenology would have been the study of the merely subjective, apparent, or superficial. But this is not the case. As Heidegger points out in section 7 of *Being and Time*, phenomenology is drawing on and employing a very different and more classical conception of the phenomenon, according to which the phenomenon is that which shows itself, that which reveals itself.[3] Phenomenology is, consequently, not a theory about the *merely* apparent, as Heidegger also pointed out in a lecture course given a few years before *Being and Time*:

> It is phenomenologically absurd to speak of the phenomenon as if it were something behind which there would be something else of which it would be a phenomenon in the sense of the appearance which represents and expresses [this something else]. A phenomenon is nothing behind which there would be something else. More accurately stated, one cannot ask for something behind the phenomenon at all, since what the phenomenon gives is precisely that something in itself.[4]

Whereas some might claim that the phenomenon is something merely subjective, a veil or smoke screen, that conceals the objectively existing reality, phenomenologists reject what might be called a two-world doctrine, i.e., the proposal that we have to make a principled distinction between the world that presents itself to and can be understood by us and the world as it is in itself. This is certainly not to deny the distinction between *mere* appearance and reality – after all, some appearances are misleading – but, for phenomenologists, this distinction is not a distinction between two separate realms (falling in the provinces of phenomenology and science, respectively), but a distinction between two modes of manifestation. It is a distinction between how the objects might appear at a superficial glance, and how they might appear in the best of circumstances, for instance as a result of a thorough scientific investigation. Indeed, phenomenologists will typically claim that the world that appears to us, be it perceptually, in our daily use, or in scientific analysis, has all the required reality and objectivity. To claim that there exists, in addition, a behind-the-scenes world, a hidden world that transcends every type of givenness, every type of evidence, and that this is the really real reality, is rejected as an empty speculative claim by the phenomenologists. In fact, they would insist that the very proposal involves a category-mistake, a misapplication and abuse of the very concept of reality. Rather than defining objective reality in terms of an inaccessible and ungraspable beyond, phenomenologists would argue that the right place to locate objectivity is in, rather than beyond, the appearing world.

Given what has been said so far, what should one conclude regarding the very scope and domain of the phenomenological investigation? What is ultimately at stake in phenomenological analyses? Are they primarily to be understood as careful investigations of consciousness? As should be clear by now, phenomenology is not primarily (or even exclusively) focused on the structure of the mind. Rather, the proper focus of phenomenological analysis is the mind–world dyad (or, as we shall eventually see, the self–other–world triad). This will become clearer the moment we consider the central concept of *intentionality*.

NOTES

1 Beauvoir, S. de (1965). *The Prime of Life*, trans. P. Green. Harmondsworth: Penguin Books: 135.
2 Husserl, E. (2001c). *Analyses Concerning Passive and Active Synthesis: Lectures on Transcendental Logic*, trans. A. Steinbock. Dordrecht: Kluwer Academic Publishers: 41.
3 Heidegger, M. (1996). *Being and Time*, trans. J. Stambaugh. Albany, NY: SUNY: 25.
4 Heidegger, M. (1985). *History of the Concept of Time: Prolegomena*, trans. T. Kisiel. Bloomington, IN: Indiana University Press: 86.

SUGGESTIONS FOR FURTHER READING

Walter Hopp, *Phenomenology: A Contemporary Introduction*. London: Routledge, 2020.
Robert Sokolowski, *Introduction to Phenomenology*. Cambridge: Cambridge University Press, 1999.
Dan Zahavi, *Husserl's Phenomenology*. Stanford, CA: Stanford University Press, 2003.

2

INTENTIONALITY

I can think about prime numbers or far-away galaxies, imagine unicorns, taste chamomile tea, fear dementors, remember events from my childhood, or recognise a photo of the Danish King. It would consequently be a fundamental mischaracterisation of my experiential life if one were to think of it simply as an amalgam of more or less intense internal sensations and feeling states. When we see, hear, remember, imagine, think, hate, or fear, our seeing, hearing, remembering, imagining, thinking, hating, and fearing is about something. Consciousness has a directedness to it, it is a consciousness of something, it is characterized by *intentionality*. Consciousness is not concerned or preoccupied with itself, but is, rather, by nature self-transcending. For phenomenologists, "intentionality" is the generic term for this pointing-beyond-itself proper to consciousness. It is, consequently, important not to confuse this sense of the term with the more familiar sense of intentionality as having a purpose in mind when one acts.

Although the notion of intentionality has a long history that stretches back at least as far as Aristotle, and although it also played a central role in medieval philosophy, it was subjected to a profound analysis in what is often considered the first major work in

DOI: 10.4324/9781003350682-4

phenomenology, Husserl's *Logical Investigations* (1900–1901). It was also a topic that Husserl kept working on for the rest of his life.

Why was the topic deemed to be of crucial importance? Because its investigation allowed for a clarification of the connection as well as of the difference between experiential subjectivity and worldly objects.

In being intentional, consciousness is not self-enclosed, but primarily occupied with objects and events that, by nature, are utterly different from consciousness itself. The birthday cake that I perceive is quite different from my perception of it. The birthday cake weighs 3 kilogrammes, can be eaten, and can be used in an act of clowning. My experience of the cake, by contrast, does not weigh anything, cannot be eaten, and cannot hit anybody in the face. And whereas the cake is not of or about anything, the perception of the cake is exactly about something, namely the cake.

It is customary to speak of intentionality as being aspectual or perspectival. One is never conscious of an object *simpliciter*, one is always conscious of an object in a particular way, be it from a certain perspective, or under a particular description. The object is always presented in a certain way to the subject. I might think of my smartphone as a means of communication, as a present I received from a friend, as an efficient way to store my music, or as a source of irritation (because it doesn't work properly), etc. But apart from intending different properties of the object, apart from varying what the object that is intended is presented *as*, one might also vary the very form of presentation itself. Instead of perceiving a table, I can also imagine it, judge it, remember it, etc. Needless to say, the same object can be intended in different ways, and the same type of intentionality can target different objects. It is possible to *doubt* "that the financial crisis will continue", to *doubt* "that the election was fair", or to *doubt* "that the climate crisis is fake news", just as it is possible to *see* "that it rains", *imagine* "that it rains", or *deny* "that it rains". Each type of intentional experience, be it a perception, an imagining, a desiring, a remembering, etc., is directed at its object in a distinctive way. A central phenomenological task is to analyse these differences in detail, and to map out the way they are systematically interrelated.

PERCEPTION AND PICTURES

In his classical analyses, Husserl emphasises the primacy of perceptual intentionality. Consider the following comparison: We might discuss which cake to buy for a birthday party. Should it be an Othello Cake or a Sachertorte? We can think and talk and be conscious of these cakes, even in their absence, i.e., even when they are not to be found in our spatial vicinity. We might also study a photo of the Othello Cake in order to discover more details about its composition and look. We remain directed at the same (type of) cake as before, but it has now gained a pictorial presence. Finally, we might buy (or bake) the cake, and see and taste it. In all three cases, we are directed at the very same (type of) cake, but the way the cake shows itself in the three cases is quite different. One possibility is to rank the intentional acts according to their ability to give us the object as directly and originally as possible. Consider first *linguistic* acts. When we simply think and talk about the cake, the cake is certainly the object of our reference, it is the cake we are thinking and talking about, but it is not given in any intuitive manner. The *pictorial* acts have a certain intuitive content, but like the linguistic acts, they intend the object indirectly. Whereas the linguistic acts intend the object via conventional representations (linguistic signs), the pictorial acts intend the object via a representation (picture) that bears a certain similarity to the object. It is only *perceptual* acts that give us the object directly. It is this type of intention which, according to Husserl, provides us with the object itself in its bodily presence.[1]

The claim, however, is not merely that perceptual intentionality presents us with the object in a privileged manner – again, compare talking about flying in a hot air balloon, seeing a video about it, or experiencing it yourself – the claim is also that perceptual intentionality is more basic than other more complex forms of intentionality, such as recollection or pictorial intentionality. When we have episodic memories, when we remember what we had for breakfast earlier in the day, we are remembering prior perceptual experiences. To that extent, recollection is founded upon and presupposes perception. When we look at pictures and see depicted objects, things get even more complicated. Consider the following example: I am visiting the Museum of Fine Arts in Vienna and now stand in front of Dürer's portrait of Emperor Maximilian. What object am I directed at? I can attend to the image-thing, i.e., the portrait as a physical object, that is, as a framed canvas with some layers of paint; I can attend to the image-object, i.e., the very pictorial representation and its aesthetic qualities and consider how successful Dürer's depiction is; or I can attend to the image-subject, i.e., that which is depicted.[2] Normally, our attention is at first drawn to the latter. I might be fascinated by Maximilian's distinct profile, by his luxurious dress, or by the pomegranate he is holding in his left hand. This might seem easy and straightforward, but is in fact no small accomplishment, since it involves a fairly complex stratified form of intentionality. To see why, consider what it means for something to be (and function as) an image of something else. How come one object depicts another object? Whereas there is no intrinsic relation between the sign and that which it signifies, the picture supposedly has certain intrinsic qualities that constrain what it can be said to depict. When combined in the right manner, the five letters c-h-a-i-r refer to a chair, but this reference is purely conventional, and might have been different. In Danish, the relevant letters are s-t-o-l. By contrast, we cannot without further ado decide that Dürer's portrait depicts a can of Heinz tomato soup. It would be a mistake, however, to think that the mere presence of a certain similarity makes one object depict another object. Regardless of how much two things look alike, it does not make one into a picture or image of the other. Two blades of grass may look quite alike, but that does not make one into a picture of the other; and whereas resemblance is a reciprocal relation, this is not the case for representation. The portrait is a picture of Maximilian, but Maximilian does not depict or represent the picture. According to Husserl's analysis of pictorial intentionality, one physical object can only come to function as a picture of something else, can only come to depict something else, if it is apprehended in a specific way by the spectator. To phrase it somewhat paradoxically, in order to see what is depicted in the picture, we both have to see and not see that which is physically in front of us. In a way, the frame functions as a kind of window into a pictorial world.[3] We have to perceive the frame and canvas, but we also have to transcend what is physically present in front of us, in order to allow the depicted to appear pictorially.

An everyday example can confirm this. If you are reading the news-paper, and come across a photo of the French President Emmanuel Macron, you are normally conscious of Macron, he is the object of your intention. But if the photo as image-object is very fuzzy and heavily pixelated, that element might force itself upon your atten-tion. Even in the best of circumstances, however, pictorial inten-tionality remains mediated and involves a peripheral awareness of the image-thing. If it did not, we would be experiencing the depicted as actually present, and would consequently be having an illusion.[4]

REPRESENTATION AND CAUSALITY

Regardless of whether we are talking about a simple case of percep-tual intentionality or a complex case where we remember having visited an art gallery where we saw X's depiction of Y, consciousness remains outward-directed, concerned and occupied with objects and events different from itself. But how is this possible? How is it that the mind can perform this extraordinary feat? As Sartre points out, it has long been taken for granted that in order to know the world we must take it in and make it part of ourselves. After all, if we see a lemon tree, we cannot actually crawl out of our heads to approach the tree. The lemon tree, on the other hand, while unable to be physically present inside our head, can affect my sensory appa-ratus, and as a result of this causal impact, a mental representation, that is, an inner sign or image of the tree, can arise in my mind. We can thus quickly reach the conclusion that what we are primarily familiar with is the internal content of consciousness.[5] On such an account, ordinary perception consequently implies two different entities, the extramental object and the intramental representation, and my access to the former is mediated and enabled by the latter.

This construal is rejected by all phenomenologists, however. Let me here just mention two of their criticisms.

The first criticism targets the introduction of a representational mediation, the second the attempt to explain intentionality on the basis of causality.

Representationalism notoriously courts scepticism: Why should awareness of one thing (an inner object) enable awareness of a quite different thing (an external object), and how should we ever be in a position to determine whether that which is internally accessible actually represents something external? After all, it is not as if we can step outside our consciousness from time to time in order to compare what is inside with what is outside. In addition, if we actually examine our perceptual experience, we should realise that it does not confront us with pictures or signs of objects – except, of course, in so far as we are perceiving paintings or photographs – but with the objects themselves. When we see a photo of the Empire State Building or Dürer's portrait of Emperor Maximilian, we are faced with a complicated form of intentionality, where our awareness of one entity (the photo or painting) allows us to be aware of another thing (the building or person). We are directed not at that which we perceive, but through it, at something else. In ordinary perception, by contrast, the perceptually given does not function as a sign or picture of something else. Indeed, if Husserl is right, if an object is to function as a picture or sign, we first have to perceive it. Only then can it, in a subsequent step, acquire its representational property. But if this is so, the representational theory of perception obviously has to be rejected, since it presupposes that which it seeks to explain.

What about causality? Is perceptual intentionality not best explained as a form of causal connection between the object of perception and the subject of perception? Could it not be that causality is the glue that connects world and mind, such that a conscious state can be said to represent (be directed at) an object, if and only if the object affects it causally? However, this rather crude account faces some obvious difficulties. When I look at a distant hill through binoculars, we would ordinarily say that the object of my perception is the hill. However, although (light reflected from) the hill might causally affect my visual system, it would certainly not be the only cause, but merely a rather distal one. Why don't I perceive (represent) the lenses of the binoculars, not to speak of the proximal stimulation of my retina? Another problem is that the notion of causality seems too coarse-grained to be able to capture the aspectual nature of intentionality. Let us assume that I enter a room and see a worn brown suitcase. The suitcase will always appear to me in a certain way. I can never see all of the suitcase (front, back, bottom, inside) simultaneously. The suitcase also appears in a particular illumination and against a specific background. It might be assumed that this can all be easily explained by the way the suitcase causally affects my visual system, but we need to consider that the suitcase will also always appear in a specific context with a specific meaning. Depending on my previous experiences and current interests, the exact same suitcase might show itself as travel equipment, as a container for old letters, as an exemplar of the thesis that all spatial objects have a backside, as a reminder of Ellis Island, or as a symbol of the current refugee crisis. To put it differently, I can relate to the very same suitcase in many different ways, practically as well as theoretically. It is not obvious that the causal impact exerted by the suitcase can account for all these differences. The most troublesome objection to the attempt to reduce intentionality to causality is, however, the following: Real existing spatial objects in my immediate physical surrounding, objects that might causally affect me, only constitute a very small part of what I can be conscious of. I can think about the backside of the moon, about square circles, unicorns, next Christmas, or the principle of non-contradiction. But how are these *absent* objects, *impossible* objects, *fictive* objects, *future* objects, or *ideal* objects supposed to affect me causally? The fact that it is possible to think about objects which do not exist seems a decisive argument against a theory that claims that an object must influence me causally if I am to be conscious of it.

As for the specific case of perceptual intentionality, phenomenologists would argue that we should stop conceiving of perceptual experience as some kind of internal movie screen that confronts us with mental representations. The taste of a lemon, the smell of coffee, the coldness of an ice cube are not qualities belonging to some spurious mental objects, but qualities of the presented objects. Instead of thinking that objects need to be internally reproduced or represented in order to be experienced, phenomenologists would argue that perceptual experience is an openness to the world that presents us with the object directly and immediately. Rather than saying that we experience representations, and rather than thinking of perceptual intentionality as a form of re-presentation, perception is best thought of as a form of presentation.

In addition, we should also give up the idea of trying to explain the mind–world relation in causal terms. Objects in the world interact causally, but the mind is not simply an object, and the peculiar nature of the mind–world relationship cannot be equated with or assimilated to the kind of causal relationship that obtains between two intra-worldly objects. Indeed, to approach the mind as if it was simply yet another object in the world would, according to phenomenologists, prevent one from disclosing, let alone clarifying, some of the most interesting aspects of consciousness, including its true epistemic and ontological significance.

As should have become clear by now, the reason why phenomenologists are interested in analysing the structure of conscious intentionality is because they want to clarify the relation between mind and world. They are not particularly concerned with the relation between the mind and the brain, and do not share the view that a proper account of intentionality is one that explains it reductively by appeal to non-intentional mechanisms and processes. Phenomenology contends that consciousness is characterised by an intrinsic and underived intentionality and would argue that meaning rather than causality plays a fundamental role. A stone might hit a window and thereby cause it to crack. But although the two objects are causally related, it doesn't make one conscious of the other, it doesn't make one be about the other. Even if I am causally affected by a cake, when I perceive it, it is not the causation that makes me perceptually aware of the cake. Rather, the cake has meaning for me, and I intend it, am directed at it, by meaning something about it.

MIND AND WORLD

There is much more to be said about intentionality. What is of importance for the present purpose is the fact that phenomenologists, by insisting on the intentional character of the mind, want to emphasise its self-transcending character. The mind is not initially and taken on its own a self-enclosed sphere that has to await a causal impact from elsewhere in order to become world-related. It is as misleading to conceive of consciousness as somehow located inside an interior sphere where it merely deals with internal representations of the world as it is to regard the world as somehow outside or external to us. It is as wrong to claim that consciousness must literally get outside itself if it is to reach the world as it is to claim that the mind must somehow absorb or digest the world in order to become aware of it. All of these proposals are equally mistaken, and all fail to realise that consciousness is neither a container nor a special place, but rather should be defined in terms of its openness. We do not at first reside inside an isolated subjective sphere in order, then, to venture out into the world from time to time. Rather the intentional openness of consciousness is an integral part of its being; its world-relatedness is part of its nature. A famous passage in Heidegger's *Being and Time* nicely captures this basic insight:

> In directing itself toward [. . .] and in grasping something, Dasein does not first go outside of the inner sphere in which it is initially encapsulated, but, rather, in its primary kind of being, it is always already "outside" together with some being encountered in the world already discovered. Nor is any inner sphere abandoned when Dasein dwells together with a being to be known and determines its character. Rather, even in this "being outside" together with its object, Dasein is "inside", correctly understood; that is, it itself exists as the being-in-the-world which knows.[6]

Heidegger doesn't speak of the intentional subject, of subjectivity or consciousness, but prefers to use the term *Dasein* (which is composed of "Da", meaning "there", and "sein", meaning "being", i.e., there-being or being-there). This terminological choice is partially motivated by his wish to avoid some of the misleading connotations that come with the traditional terms, and partially in order to empha-sise that our very being is to be located in and involved with the world. Indeed, what a phenomenological investigation reveals is that traditional categories such as inner and outer cannot adequately cap-ture the relation between Dasein and world. Since Dasein is always already dwelling among things, it has no outside, which is also why it is nonsensical to talk of it as having an inside. Similar ideas can be found in Husserl, who argues that the facile divide between inside and outside is inappropriate for a proper understanding of intention-ality, and that the subject is neither in the world nor outside it, just as the world is neither in the subject nor outside of it. The very division between inner–outer is precisely one with which phenom-enology plays havoc. As Merleau-Ponty puts it: "The world is entirely on the inside, and I am entirely outside of myself".[7]

If we for a moment return to pictorial intentionality, the point of the example was not merely to highlight how it differs from perceptual intentionality, but also to show that what might appear as a fairly simple accomplishment – seeing a picture of the Eiffel Tower – actually harbours quite a complex intentional interplay. Normally, we take pictures for granted and remain oblivious to our own intentional contribution. But pictures do not simply exist naturally. There would be no pictures in a mindless universe. Objects only come to function as pictures due to a special intentional accomplishment. The radical phenomenological claim is now that this also holds true more generally. As Husserl writes in an early text:

> [T]he objects of which we are "conscious", are not simply *in* consciousness as in a box, so that they can merely be found in it and snatched at in it; [. . .] they are first *constituted* as being what they are for us, and as what they count as for us, in varying forms of objective intention.[8]

In phenomenological texts, the term "constitution" is a technical one. Constitution doesn't mean creation. Consciousness does not create the objects it constitutes out of nothing. Nor is it their source, in the sense that they can somehow be deduced from or explained by its operations. It is not as if the fact that water is composed of hydrogen and oxygen, rather than helium and xenon, is somehow to be explained with reference to consciousness. To speak of constituting consciousness is not to speak of a mind that shapes the world in its own image; rather, constitution must be understood as a process that allows for objects to appear or manifest themselves meaningfully, i.e., it is a process that permits that which is constituted to appear, to manifest, and present itself as what it is. And this process is precisely one that in significant ways involves consciousness.

Normally, we live a life of self-forgetfulness where we are absorbed in worldly events. We focus on the object that appears and do not attend to the object as it appears. We do not pause to ask or examine how things can appear to us in the way they do, and with the meaning that they have. But if we are to philosophically comprehend what it means for something to be a perceived object, a remembered event, a judged state of affairs, we cannot ignore the kinds of intentionality (the perceiving, the remembering, and the judging) that reveal these objects to us. Although we tend to ignore the modes of givenness in daily life, the task of phenomenology was from the beginning to break with the naivety of daily life and to call attention to and investigate the correlation between act and object, between *cogito* and *cogitatum*.

We need to recognise the difference between the intentional experience and the intentional object. But the fact that they are different does not entail that they are not essentially related. A proper phenomenological investigation of intentionality should not merely consider the subjective side – say, the perceptual or emotional experience – but must also investigate their objective correlates – the perceived or desired object. The same holds true in reverse. We cannot analyse the intentional object properly without considering its subjective correlate, the intentional act. A main concern of phenomenology was precisely to account for this relation between the subjective and the objective. For Husserl, the greatest and most important problems in phenomenology were related to the question of how objectivities of different kinds, from the pre-scientific ones to those of the highest scientific dignity, are constituted by consciousness. Indeed, the task of phenomenology is to inquire "in the most comprehensive universality, into how Objective unities of any region and category are 'constituted in the manner peculiar to consciousness'".[9]

We are now approaching a core feature of phenomenological thinking. The reason for the phenomenological interest in intentionality is not primarily due to a narrow concern with and interest in subjective experiences per se. The argument is rather that if we really wish to understand the status of physical objects, mathematical models, chemical processes, social relations, cultural products, etc., then we need to understand how they can appear as what they are and with the meaning they have. In order to do that, we also have to consider the subject(s) for whom they appear. When we encounter perceived, judged, evaluated objects, a thorough philosophical examination of these objects will lead us to the experiential structures that these modes of appearance are correlated with. We will be led to the acts of presentation, perception, judgment, and valuation, and thereby to the subject(s) that the object as appearing must necessarily be understood in relation to.

By adopting the phenomenological attitude, we thematise the givenness of objects. But we do not simply focus on the objects precisely as they are given; we also focus on the structure of the respective object-experience, thereby becoming aware of our subjective accomplishments and of the intentionality that is at play in order for the objects to appear as they do. When we investigate appearing objects, we also disclose ourselves as those to whom objects appear. The topic of phenomenological analyses is, consequently, not a worldless subject, and phenomenology does not ignore the world in favour of consciousness. Rather, phenomenology is interested in consciousness because it is world-disclosing. It is in order to understand how the world can appear in the way it does, and with the validity and meaning it has, that phenomenology comes to investigate the disclosing performance of intentional consciousness. Rather than merely amounting to a limited exploration of the psychological domain, an in-depth investigation of intentionality is taken to pave the way for a proper understanding of reality and objectivity.

Indeed, one of the reasons why the theory of intentionality occupies centre stage in Husserl's thinking is precisely because he considers a study of the world-directedness of consciousness to provide us with insights into not only the structure of subjectivity, but also into the nature of objectivity. That something like a conscious appropriation of the world is possible does not merely tell us something about consciousness, but also about the world. But, of course, this way of discussing consciousness, as the constitutive dimension that makes any worldly manifestation possible, as the "place" in which the world can reveal and articulate itself, is quite different from any attempt to treat it scientifically as merely yet another (psychical or physical) object in the world.

By insisting on the fact that mind and world must be explored simultaneously, phenomenology offers a perspective that straddles or undermines the traditional distinction between epistemology and ontology. Traditionally, one has distinguished the question of how we come to understand and have knowledge of the world, from questions pertaining to the nature of reality. A tempting and easy move is to insist that whereas an answer to the former question might in various ways appeal to and involve subjective and experiential processes, the answer to the latter question has quite deliberately to subtract any subjective contribution we make in order to account for reality from "a view from nowhere". By focusing on the phenomena, however, phenomenology is at once analysing our way of understanding and experiencing the world, and at the same time, the objects and their modes of appearance. This is why Heidegger in *Being and Time* can write that ontology is only possible as phenomenology, and that the analysis of our being-in-the-world is the key to every ontological exploration.[10]

More generally speaking, phenomenologists would dispute that the relation between world and subjectivity is merely accidental, as if they were like two pieces of Lego, which can either be stuck together or separated. The lesson of intentionality is that the mind is essentially open, and that reality is essentially manifestable. For something to count as real, it must in principle be something we can encounter, though the mode of encounter can vary: Perceptual acquaintance, practical engagement, and scientific investigation are merely some of the possible forms. To reject this idea, and to claim that the moon, a neuron, a deck of cards, or a communal ritual have a unfathomable and hidden true being, that what they really are is something completely divorced from any context of use, network of meaning, or theoretical framework, and that whatever experiential and theoretical perspective we might adopt on them is consequently bound to miss its target, is not only a deeply obfuscating claim, but also one that is epistemologically naive. On what basis and from what perspective could such a claim ever be justified? We cannot look sideways at our experiences in order to see to what extent they match with reality. This is so, not because such a view is extremely hard to reach, but because the very idea of such a view is nonsensical. Any understanding of reality is by definition perspectival. Effacing our perspective does not bring us any closer to the world. It merely prevents us from understanding anything about the world at all.

REALISM AND IDEALISM

By insisting on the interdependence and inseparability of mind and world, phenomenologists are not reducing the world to intramental modifications or constructions. They are combining the claim that the world is different from the mind with the claim that world is also related to the mind, and vice versa. A pregnant formulation of this idea can be found in an early text by Sartre:

Husserl persistently affirmed that one cannot dissolve things in consciousness. You see this tree, to be sure. But you see it just where it is: at the side of the road, in the midst of the dust, alone and writhing in the heat, eight miles from the Mediterranean coast. It could not enter into your consciousness, for it is not of the same nature as consciousness. [. . .] But Husserl is not a realist: this tree on its bit of parched earth is not an absolute that would subsequently enter into communication with me. Consciousness and the world are given at one stroke: essentially external to consciousness, the world is nevertheless essentially relative to consciousness.[11]

The scholarly literature is filled with discussions of whether such a view makes phenomenology committed to a form of philosophical idealism. Levinas once remarked that Husserl's idealism is not a theory about how the subject is closed in upon itself and only knows its own states, but a theory about how the subject, qua intentional, is open to everything.[12] Much consequently depends on the definitions used. If one defines idealism as the view that the subject is only aware of its own subjective states, and if realism is then the view that we are directly aware of objects in the world, objects with a totally different kind of being than the mind, Husserl might be more of a realist than a traditional idealist. As previously noted, however, there is no question that the phenomenologists are opposed to objectivism, i.e., to the view that reality is what it is completely independently of any experiencer, and that our cognitive apprehension of reality is, at best, a faithful mirroring of a pre-existing world.

This is not only Husserl's view. Heidegger and Merleau-Ponty both deny the self-contained nature of the mind and argue that it is intrinsically world-involved. In addition, however, they also defend the reverse claim, and argue that the world is tied to the mind. To put it differently, both would argue that the relation between mind and world is an internal relation, a relation constitutive of its relata, and not an external one of causality. As Heidegger writes in the lecture course *The Basic Problems of Phenomenology* from 1927:

> World exists—that is, it is—only if Dasein exists, only if there is Dasein. Only if world is there, if Dasein exists as being-in-the-world, is there understanding of being, and only if this understanding exists are intraworldly beings unveiled as extant and handy. World-understanding as Dasein-understanding is self-understanding. Self and world belong together in the single entity, the Dasein. Self and world are not two beings, like subject and object, or like I and thou, but self and world are the basic determination of the Dasein itself in the unity of the structure of being-in-the-world.[13]

A similar commitment to the interdependence of mind and world is found in Merleau-Ponty, who towards the end of *Phenomenology of Perception* declares:

> The world is inseparable from the subject, but from a subject who is nothing but a project of the world; and the subject is inseparable from the world, but from a world that it itself projects. The subject is being-in-the-world and the world remains "subjective", since its texture and its articulations are sketched out by the subject's movement of transcendence.[14]

The focus of phenomenology is on the intersection between mind and world, neither of which can be understood in separation from each other. We are what we are as a function of our world-involvement, and the world understood as the fundamental context of meaning is also only what it is because of our involvement with it. To ask what one is without the other is like asking what a background is in itself, independently of the foreground.

NOTES

1   Husserl, E. (1982). *Ideas Pertaining to a Pure Phenomenology and to a Phenomenological Philosophy. First Book. General Introduction to a Pure Phenomenology*, trans. F. Kersten. The Hague: Martinus Nijhoff: 92–93; Husserl, E. (2001b). *Logical Investigations I–II*, trans. J.N. Findlay. London: Routledge: II/260.

2   Husserl, E. (2005). *Phantasy, Image Consciousness, and Memory (1898–1925)*, trans. J.B. Brough. Dordrecht: Springer: 21.

3 Husserl, E. (2005). *Phantasy, Image Consciousness, and Memory (1898–1925)*, trans. J.B. Brough. Dordrecht: Springer: 133–134.

4 If one gets too absorbed when watching a horror movie, this might happen. Importantly, however, the specific aesthetic attitude requires that the distinction between fiction and reality is maintained. The spectator, who is so absorbed and enthralled by a performance of Shakespeare's *Romeo and Juliet* that he calls out for a doctor when he sees Romeo drink the poison, has missed something essential.

5 Sartre, J.-P. (1970). Intentionality: A fundamental idea of Husserl's phenomenology. *Journal of the British Society for Phenomenology* 1(2): 4.

6 Heidegger, M. (1996). *Being and Time*, trans. J. Stambaugh. Albany, NY: SUNY: 58. When quoting from Stambaugh's translation of *Being and Time*, the translation will throughout be modified such that Da-sein is rendered as Dasein.

7 Merleau-Ponty, M. (2012). *Phenomenology of Perception*, trans. D.A. Landes. London: Routledge: 430.

8 Husserl, E. (2001b). *Logical Investigations I–II*, trans. J.N. Findlay. London: Routledge: I/275.

9 Husserl, E. (1982). *Ideas Pertaining to a Pure Phenomenology and to a Phenomenological Philosophy. First Book. General Introduction to a Pure Phenomenology*, trans. F. Kersten. The Hague: Martinus Nijhoff: 209.

10 Heidegger, M. (1996). *Being and Time*, trans. J. Stambaugh. Albany, NY: SUNY: 31.

11 Sartre, J.-P. (1970). Intentionality: A fundamental idea of Husserl's phenomenology. *Journal of the British Society for Phenomenology* 1(2): 4.

12 Levinas, E. (1998). *Discovering Existence with Husserl*, trans. R.A. Cohen and M.B. Smith. Evanston, IL: Northwestern University Press: 69.

13 Heidegger, M. (1982). *The Basic Problems of Phenomenology*, trans. A. Hofstadter. Bloomington, IN: Indiana University Press: 297.

14 Merleau-Ponty, M. (2012). *Phenomenology of Perception*, trans. D.A. Landes. London: Routledge: 454.

SUGGESTIONS FOR FURTHER READING

Maxime Doyon, *Phenomenology and the Norms of Perception*. Oxford: Oxford University Press, 2024.

John J. Drummond, "Intentionality without representationalism." In D. Zahavi (ed.), *The Oxford Handbook of Contemporary Phenomenology* (pp. 115–133). Oxford: Oxford University Press, 2012.

Hanne Jacobs (ed.), *The Husserlian Mind*. London: Routledge, 2021.

Jean-Paul Sartre, "Intentionality: A fundamental idea of Husserl's phenomenology." *Journal of the British Society for Phenomenology* 1(2), 1970, 4–5.

3

METHODOLOGICAL CONSIDERATIONS

One of the most controversial and debated issues in phenomenology concerns that of method. What is the phenomenological method, if there is one? The question is controversial, not only because of widespread disagreements, and the quite disparate answers given, but also because Husserl's methodological steps are one of the most misunderstood aspects of his phenomenology, not only by its critics, but also by well-intended sympathisers.

EPOCHÉ AND REDUCTION

Husserl is well known for having insisted that certain methodological steps are required if phenomenology is to accomplish its designated task. Indeed, he even claimed that anybody who disregarded these steps would have no chance of comprehending what phenomenology was all about.[1] But what was he referring to? Let me focus on two well-known features. In *Logical Investigations*, Husserl declared: "We can absolutely not rest content with 'mere words' [. . .]. Meanings inspired only by remote, confused, inauthentic intuitions – if by any intuitions at all – are not enough: we must go back to the 'things themselves'".[2] In later works, Husserl also insisted on the need for a particular bracketing or suspension, the performance of

DOI: 10.4324/9781003350682-5

what he calls the *epoché*. But what is it that has to be bracketed or suspended, and why should such a procedure allow us to return to the things themselves? This is where the views diverge. On one interpretation, the return to the things themselves is a turning away from theories, interpretations, and constructions. What we have to bracket is our preconceived ideas, our habits of thoughts, our prejudices, and theoretical assumptions. Rather than arriving at the scene with a lot of theoretical baggage, the task of phenomenology is to effectuate an unprejudiced turn towards the objects. We should arrive at the scene with an open mind, in order to let the objects reveal themselves as what they are. We should focus on the things as they are encountered in experience, not on how we thought they were, and then base our definitions on careful descriptions. On this reading, phenomenology is very much a descriptive rather than deductive or speculative enterprise, the core of which is its rigorous intuitive method. Sometimes the description in question is taken to be one that seeks to disregard the particularity of the object in order to allow for a grasp of its essential features. At other times, the claim is that such a method should be as detailed as possible in order to respect and grasp the uniqueness of the particular phenomenon under investigation. One early (pre-phenomenological) articulation of this ambition can be found in Flaubert:

> We have fallen into the habit of remembering, whenever we use our eyes, what people before us have thought of the things we are looking at. Even the slightest thing contains a little that is unknown. We must find it. To describe a blazing fire or a tree in a plain, we must remain before that fire or that tree until they no longer resemble for us any other tree or any other fire.[3]

There is also another way to interpret the epoché, however. On this reading, what has to be bracketed or disregarded is not only traditional theories and prejudices, but also, and even more importantly, our habitual and natural preoccupation with worldly objects and events. The aim of phenomenology is to reveal aspects and dimensions of our subjective lives that are standardly overlooked due to our focus on and concern with objects. Indeed, on this account, the main goal of phenomenology is to expand our scope of attention such that we can thematise and describe hitherto unnoticed aspects of inner experience, which is also why critics as well as supporters have been led to the conclusion that phenomenology has many affinities with both introspective psychology and mindfulness practice.

Both interpretations are mistaken. It is not that they do not contain some elements of truth, but they miss the important part. Phenomenology is neither a turn toward the object, nor a return to the subject. In addition, it is a mistake to see the main ambition of phenomenology as being that of providing detailed descriptions. The problem with all these interpretations is not only that they fail to adequately capture the scope of the phenomenological analysis – as has already been highlighted, the aim of the phenomenological analysis is not to investigate either the object or the subject, either the world or the mind, but to investigate both in their interrelation or correlation – they also fail to recognise the properly philosophical nature of phenomenology. It is no coincidence that a purely descriptive endeavour devoid of systematic ambitions was dismissed by both Husserl and Scheler as mere "picture-book phenomenology".[4] Simply amassing various descriptions, be they of individual experiences – this is what I am feeling here and now – or of particular objects, or of their more invariant essential structures, is a poor substitute for the systematic and argumentative work that is being done by phenomenological philosophers. In short, to claim that the virtue of phenomenology is that by being attentive to how things appear it allows us to capture, say, a sunrise or a coffee aroma in all its richness, is to miss in a quite fundamental way what is really at stake in phenomenology.

But what is, then, the correct interpretation? Before proposing an answer, let me briefly consider yet another misinterpretation which has also been quite influential. According to this interpretation, the performance of the epoché makes it clear that phenomenology, rather than being a metaphysical doctrine, is a methodological or metaphilosophical endeavour. What is that supposed to mean? The idea is that what we, as phenomenologists, need to bracket and exclude from consideration is the actually existing world. By adopting the phenomenological attitude, we focus on the phenomena, on how things appear, on what they mean, and how they matter to us. This is not to say that we only focus on experience, and do not include the objects of experience, but the latter, the seen table, the touched petal, the heard melody, are considered merely insofar as they figure in our experience. Whether they really exist or not is phenomenologically irrelevant.

On this interpretation, the real purpose of the phenomenological bracketing is, consequently, to limit the scope of the investigation. There are simply certain issues that are excluded from consideration, certain questions that we as phenomenologists are not supposed to engage with. We might believe that we are directed at something extra-mental, something transcendent, something that is not contained in consciousness, and as phenomenologists, we should investigate this belief and our experiences of natural objects, artefacts, other people, works of arts, social institutions, etc., but we are not entitled to say anything about the being of these entities themselves. As a phenomenologist, I can claim that I experience a lemon, that a lemon is appearing, that it seems as if there is a lemon in front of me, but I cannot as a phenomenologist affirm that there really is a lemon. To do the latter would be to make an illegitimate transition from phenomenology, from a concern with how things appear and what meaning they have for me, to metaphysics, to a concern with reality and real existence.

As said, this (mis)interpretation has proven very influential. One problem it faces, however, is that both Heidegger and Merleau-Ponty, to mention just a few of the post-Husserlian phenomenologists, are quite explicit about their ontological commitments, about the extent to which their phenomenological work has a bearing on being. As Heidegger declares, "there is no ontology *alongside* a phenomenology. Rather, *scientific ontology is nothing but phenomenology*".[5] One way to cope with this challenge is to argue that phenomenology underwent a radical transformation after Husserl. Whereas his conception of phenomenology did involve the aforementioned constrains, later phenomenologists abandoned his methodological moves and radically transformed the entire enterprise. Plenty of books have been written on the controversial relationship between Husserlian phenomenology and post-Husserlian existential or hermeneutical phenomenology, and it would lead too far in this context to address the relationship in any detail. Let me be quite open about my own take on the matter, however. I am unequivocally on the side of those who defend the continuity thesis, and who think that there is something like a phenomenological tradition with a set of common themes and concerns that have united and continue to unite its proponents.

The most direct way to defend this interpretation is by showing that Husserl remained interested in and preoccupied with the world and with true being, and that the purpose of the epoché is not to bracket either from consideration. But again, how should it then be understood? Well first of all, as Husserl writes in *Ideas I*, the epoché is

not to be mistaken for the one which positivism requires [. . .]. It is not now a matter of excluding all prejudices that cloud the pure objectivity of research, not a matter of constituting a science "free of theories", "free of metaphysics".[6]

Rather, as Beauvoir rightly points out, Husserl's aim is to suspend "all affirmation concerning the mode of reality of the external world" in order to avoid "the errors of dogmatism".[7] To put it differently, the proper way to interpret the epoché is to see it as involving not an exclusion of reality, but rather a suspension of a particular dogmatic *attitude* towards reality, an attitude that is operative not only in the positive sciences, but also permeates our daily pre-theoretical life. Indeed, the attitude is so fundamental and pervasive that Husserl calls it the *natural attitude*. What is the attitude about? It is about simply taking it for granted that the world we encounter in experience also exists independently of us. Regardless of how natural and obvious it might be to think of reality as a self-subsisting entity, if philosophy is supposed to amount to a radical form of critical elucidation, it cannot simply take this kind of dogmatic realism for granted. If philosophy is to deserve its credentials as a form of radical questioning, it cannot simply prejudice the answer beforehand. On the contrary, if we are to adopt the phenomenological attitude and engage in phenomenological philosophising, we must take a step back from our naive and unexamined immersion in the world, and suspend our deep-seated belief in the mind-independent existence of that world. By suspending this attitude, and by thematising the fact that reality is always revealed and examined from some perspective or another, the nature of reality is not lost from sight, but is for the first time made accessible for philosophical inquiry.

But why is it, then, that many have interpreted the epoché as involving an abstention from ontological claims, a disregard for questions concerning being? Husserl himself is partly to blame for some of the misinterpretations. Consider, for instance, his discussion in section 52 of *Crisis*, where Husserl initially writes that the epoché brackets all worldly interests:

> Any interest in the being, actuality, or nonbeing of the world, i.e., any interest theoretically oriented toward knowledge of the world, and even any interest which is practical in the usual sense, with its dependence on the presuppositions of its situational truths, is forbidden.[8]

But, as he then explains one page later, this initial presentation is misleading:

> In the reorientation of the epoché nothing is lost, none of the interests and ends of world-life, and thus also none of the ends of knowledge. But for all these things their essential subjective correlates are exhibited, and thus the full and true ontic meaning of objective being, and thus of all objective truth, is set forth.[9]

Indeed, as he further explains, one of the most common misunderstandings of the epoché is that it involves a "turning-away" from "all natural human life-interests".[10] In reality, however, the so-called exclusion of the world is not an exclusion of the world, but an exclusion of a certain naive prejudice concerning the metaphysical status of the world. In short, the phenomenologist must cease to posit the world naively.[11] The world is not lost as a result of the epoché. The latter doesn't involve a suspension of the being of the world, but rather aims to remove certain blinders that will allow for a discovery of the fundamental correlation between mind and world. Indeed, Husserl is quite emphatic about the fact that by adopting the phenomenological attitude and by engaging in phenomenological reflection, we are supposed to be expanding, rather than constraining, our field of research. In *Crisis*, Husserl even compares the performance of the epoché to the transition from a two-dimensional to a three-dimensional life.[12] By performing the epoché we are supposed to effectuate a kind of gestalt shift, a change of perspective that enlarges our understanding by enabling new insights.

Strictly speaking, however, the epoché is only the first step, the gate of entry. It must be followed by what Husserl calls the *transcendental reduction*. By first bracketing or suspending the natural attitude, by no longer simply taking reality as the unquestioned point of departure, we instead pay attention to how and as what worldly objects are given to us. But, in doing so, in analysing how and as what any object presents itself to us, we also come to discover the intentional acts and experiential structures in relation to which any appearing object must necessarily be understood. We come to appreciate our own subjective accomplishments and contributions, and the intentionality that is at play in order for worldly objects to appear in the way they do and with the validity and meaning that they have. When Husserl talks of the transcendental reduction, what he has in mind is precisely the systematic analysis of this correlation between subjectivity and world. This is a more prolonged analysis that *leads* from the natural sphere *back to* (*re-ducere*) its transcendental foundation.[13] Both epoché and transcendental reduction can, consequently, be seen as elements in a philosophical reflection, the purpose of which is to liberate us from our natural(istic) dogmatism and make us aware of our own constitutive involvement, of the extent to which we are all involved in the process of constitution.

TRANSCENDENTAL PHILOSOPHY

By insisting on the indispensability of this kind of reflective move, Husserl is affirming that he belongs to a tradition in philosophy that is called *transcendental philosophy*. In this philosophical approach, the aim is not to conduct any straightforward first-order investigation of worldly objects in order to disclose new facts, as if the philosopher were like a botanist or marine biologist. A proper philosophical exploration of the nature of reality does not consist of inventorying the contents of the universe, but in accounting for what it means for something to count as real. Rather than simply naively assuming the ready-made character of the objective world, the philosophical task is to elucidate how something like objectivity is possible in the first place. How does the world come to acquire its character as true and objective? How is it that the world can be given in experience as transcending that very experience?

When we adopt the phenomenological attitude, we do not turn our attention away from the world and towards our own experiential life, we do not turn the gaze inwards in order to examine the happenings in a private interior sphere. We continue to be concerned with the worldly object, but we now no longer consider it naively; rather, we focus on it precisely as it is intended and given, i.e., as a correlate of experience. We pay attention to how and as what worldly objects are given to us. Husserl's interest in consciousness is due to the fact that it is world-disclosing; rather than merely being an *object in the world*, it is also a *subject for the world*, i.e., a necessary condition of possibility for any entity to appear as an object in the way it does and with the meaning it has.

Rather than merely amounting to a limited exploration of the psychological domain, the aim of phenomenology is, consequently, to offer a proper account of reality and objectivity. To construe Husserlian phenomenology in such a way that being and reality are topics left for other disciplines would neither respect nor reflect Husserl's own assertions on the matter. As he declares in section 23 of *Cartesian Meditations* (1931), the topics of existence and non-existence, of being and non-being, are all-embracing themes for phenomenology.[14]

Rather than making reality disappear from view, the epoché and reduction are precisely what allow reality to be investigated philosophically. In his early lecture course, *History of the Concept of Time: Prolegomena*, Heidegger discussed Husserl's phenomenological methodology and, at one point, offered the following quite acute characterisation:

> This bracketing of the entity takes nothing away from the entity itself, nor does it purport to assume that the entity is not. This reversal of perspective has rather the sense of making the being of the entity present. This phenomenological suspension of the transcendent thesis has but the sole function of making the entity present in regard to its being. The term "suspension" is thus always misunderstood when it is thought that in suspending the thesis of existence and by doing so, phenomenological reflection simply has nothing more to do with the entity. Quite the contrary: in an extreme and unique way, what really is at issue now is the determination of the being of the very entity.[15]

Husserl repeatedly insisted that one will have no chance of comprehending what phenomenology is all about if one considers the epoché and the transcendental reduction as irrelevant peculiarities. But what about later phenomenologists? It is indisputable that neither Heidegger nor Merleau-Ponty made many references to the epoché and the reduction. But is this because they rejected Husserl's methodology, or is it because they simply took it for granted? In sections 27–33 of *Ideas I*, Husserl describes the natural attitude in detail and argues that the fundamental structures of our relation to the world, as well as the special character of our own subjectivity, will remain concealed as long as we simply continue to live naively in the natural pre-philosophical attitude. It is by suspending our natural attitude that we discover that there is more to our subjectivity than merely being yet another object in the world.

If we move from *Ideas I* to *Being and Time*, we will find Heidegger arguing in a somewhat similar manner. For Heidegger, everyday existence is characterised by self-forgetfulness and self-objectification. We all tend to let our own self-understanding be guided by and, therefore, covered over by our commonsensical understanding of worldly matters.[16] Phenomenology can be described as a struggle against this levelling self-understanding. This is why Heidegger in *Being and Time* writes that the phenomenological analysis is characterised by a certain violence, since its disclosure of the being of Dasein is only to be won in direct confrontation with Dasein's own tendency to cover things up. In fact, it must be wrested and captured from Dasein.[17] Heidegger also talks of how our ordinary life is a life led according to conventional norms and standards. Everything is already understood and interpreted by others, and we all tend to uncritically take over prevailing judgments and valuations. By leaving all of these unquestioned, we feel safe and at home, and have no real incentive to start asking fundamental and unsettling questions. But certain events – for instance, being overwhelmed by anxiety – can make everyday familiarity collapse, can make even the most familiar of places unfamiliar and uncanny. In such situations, it will be impossible to simply continue to rely on conventional interpretations of the world.[18] To that extent, anxiety can be seen as a happening that might rupture our natural thoughtlessness and propel us into philosophical questioning.

If we next consider *Phenomenology of Perception*, we find Merleau-Ponty writing as follows:

Because we are through and through related to the world, the only way for us to catch sight of ourselves is by suspending this movement, by refusing to be complicit with it (or as Husserl often says, to see it *ohne mitzu-machen* [without taking part]), or again, to put it out of play. This is not because we renounce the certainties of common sense and of the natural attitude – on the contrary, these are the constant theme of philosophy – but rather because, precisely as the presuppositions of every thought, they are "taken for granted" and they pass by unnoticed, and because we must abstain from them for a moment in order to awaken them and to make them appear. Perhaps the best formulation of the reduction is the one offered by Husserl's assistant Eugen Fink when he spoke of a "wonder" before the world. Reflection does not withdraw from the world toward the unity of consciousness as the foundation of the world; rather, it steps back in order to see transcendences spring forth and it loosens the intentional threads that connect us to the world in order to make them appear; it alone is conscious of the world because it reveals the world as strange and paradoxical.[19]

In the same book, we will also find Merleau-Ponty arguing that we need to break with our familiar acceptance of the world if we are to understand the latter properly, and that a proper investigation of consciousness cannot take place as long as the absolute (i.e., mind-independent) existence of the world is left unquestioned.[20]

Neither Heidegger nor Merleau-Ponty would have accepted the claim that the task of phenomenology is to describe objects or experiences as precisely and meticulously as possible, nor do they take it to be concerned with an investigation of phenomena in all their factual diversity. For both of them, philosophy is characterised by a quite different stance than the one found in the positive sciences. The epoché and the reduction are Husserl's terms for the reflective move that is needed in order to attain the stance of philosophical thinking. Despite the disagreements they might have with various details of Husserl's programme, both Heidegger and Merleau-Ponty are fully committed to this reflective move. For both Merleau-Ponty and Heidegger, positive science takes certain ideas about the mind-independent nature of reality for granted and seems to consider such ideas exempt from critical scrutiny. But the aim of phenomenology is to question such objectivism, and to investigate all objects, scientific findings, cultural accomplishments, social institutions, etc., with an eye to how they present or manifest themselves to us. If we, as phenomenologists, are to engage with fundamental ontological questions, we have, according to Heidegger, to proceed via an investigation of Dasein's understanding of being; that is, we have to investigate being "in so far as it stands within the intelligibility of Dasein".[21]

The relation between Husserl and the post-Husserlian phenomenologists continues to be controversial. Opinions diverge widely regarding the extent to which figures like Heidegger and Merleau-Ponty remained indebted to Husserl. Whereas Carman has argued that "Heidegger's fundamental ontology cannot be understood as a mere supplement or continuation, let alone 'translation', of Husserl's philosophy",[22] Merleau-Ponty declared that the whole of *Being and Time* was nothing but an explication of Husserl's notion of the life-world.[23] And whereas Merleau-Ponty himself repeatedly emphasised his indebtedness to Husserl and occasionally presented his own work as an attempt to unearth the implications of Husserl's late philosophy and to think his "unthought thought",[24] numerous Merleau-Ponty scholars have insisted that the Husserl Merleau-Ponty found reason to praise was primarily an extrapolation of Merleau-Ponty's own philosophy.[25]

There are undoubtedly significant differences between Husserl, Heidegger, and Merleau-Ponty. Whatever influence Husserl exerted on Heidegger and Merleau-Ponty, the latter two were also indebted to other seminal figures in the philosophical tradition, including Aristotle, Descartes, Kierkegaard, Nietzsche, Bergson, and Sartre. But much of Heidegger's and Merleau-Ponty's disagreement with Husserl takes place within a horizon of shared assumptions. It is an immanent criticism, a criticism internal to phenomenology, and not a break with or general rejection of it. To put it differently, in order to understand and appreciate the *phenomenological* aspect of Heidegger's and Merleau-Ponty's thinking, a familiarity with Husserl remains indispensable.

NOTES

1 Husserl, E. (1982). *Ideas Pertaining to a Pure Phenomenology and to a Phenomenological Philosophy. First Book. General Introduction to a Pure Phenomenology,* trans. F. Kersten. The Hague: Martinus Nijhoff: 211.

2 Husserl, E. (2001b). *Logical Investigations I–II,* trans. J.N. Findlay. London: Routledge: I/168.

3 Quoted in Steegmuller, F. (1949). *Maupassant: A Lion in the Path.* London: Macmillan: 60.

4 Spiegelberg, H. (1965). *The Phenomenological Movement.* The Hague: Martinus Nijhoff: 170; Scheler, M. (1973). *Formalism in Ethics and Non-Formal Ethics of Values: A New Attempt Toward a Foundation of an Ethical Personalism,* trans. M.S. Frings and R.L. Funk. Evanston, IL: Northwestern University Press: xix.

5 Heidegger, M. (1985). *History of the Concept of Time: Prolegomena,* trans. T. Kisiel. Bloomington, IN: Indiana University Press: 72.

6 Husserl, E. (1982). *Ideas Pertaining to a Pure Phenomenology and to a Phenomenological Philosophy. First Book. General Introduction to a Pure Phenomenology,* trans. F. Kersten. The Hague: Martinus Nijhoff: 62.

7 Beauvoir, S. de (2018). *The Ethics of Ambiguity,* trans. B. Frechtman. New York, NY: Open Road Media: 13.

8 Husserl, E. (1970). *The Crisis of European Sciences and Transcendental Phenomenology: An Introduction to Phenomenological Philosophy,* trans. D. Carr. Evanston, IL: Northwestern University Press: 175.

9 Husserl, E. (1970). *The Crisis of European Sciences and Transcendental Phenomenology: An Introduction to Phenomenological Philosophy,* trans. D. Carr. Evanston, IL: Northwestern University Press: 176.

10 Husserl, E. (1970). *The Crisis of European Sciences and Transcendental Phenomenology: An Introduction to Phenomenological Philosophy,* trans. D. Carr. Evanston, IL: Northwestern University Press: 176.

11 Husserl, E. (2002). *Zur phänomenologischen Reduktion: Texte aus dem Nachlass (1926–1935),* ed. by S. Luft. Husserliana 34. Dordrecht: Kluwer Academic Publishers: 21.

12 Husserl, E. (1970). *The Crisis of European Sciences and Transcendental Phenomenology: An Introduction to Phenomenological Philosophy,* trans. D. Carr. Evanston, IL: Northwestern University Press: 119.

13 Husserl, E. (1960). *Cartesian Meditations: An Introduction to Phenomenology,* trans. D. Cairns. The Hague: Martinus Nijhoff: 21.

14 Husserl, E. (1960). *Cartesian Meditations: An Introduction to Phenomenology,* trans. D. Cairns. The Hague: Martinus Nijhoff: 56.

15 Heidegger, M. (1985). *History of the Concept of Time: Prolegomena,* trans. T. Kisiel. Bloomington, IN: Indiana University Press: 99.

16 Heidegger, M. (1996). *Being and Time,* trans. J. Stambaugh. Albany, NY: SUNY: 18.

17 Heidegger, M. (1996). *Being and Time*, trans. J. Stambaugh. Albany, NY: SUNY: 187, 287, 289.

18 Heidegger, M. (1996). *Being and Time*, trans. J. Stambaugh. Albany, NY: SUNY: 175.

19 Merleau-Ponty, M. (2012). *Phenomenology of Perception*, trans. D.A. Landes. London: Routledge: lxxvii.

20 Merleau-Ponty, M. (2012). *Phenomenology of Perception*, trans. D.A. Landes. London: Routledge: 59–60.

21 Heidegger, M. (1996). *Being and Time*, trans. J. Stambaugh. Albany, NY: SUNY: 142.

22 Carman, T. (2003). *Heidegger's Analytic: Interpretation, Discourse and Authenticity in Being and Time*. Cambridge: Cambridge University Press: 62.

23 Merleau-Ponty, M. (2012). *Phenomenology of Perception*, trans. D.A. Landes. London: Routledge: lxx.

24 Merleau-Ponty, M. (1964a). *Signs*, trans. R.C. McClearly. Evanston, IL: Northwestern University Press: 160.

25 Madison, G.B. (1981). *The Phenomenology of Merleau-Ponty*. Athens, OH: Ohio University: 170; Dillon, M.C. (1988). *Merleau-Ponty's Ontology*. 2nd edn. Evanston, IL: Northwestern University Press: 27.

SUGGESTIONS FOR FURTHER READING

John D. Caputo, "The question of being and transcendental phenomenology: Reflections on Heidegger's relationship to Husserl." *Research in Phenomenology* 7(1), 1977, 84–105.

Steven Crowell, "Heidegger and Husserl: The matter and method of philosophy." In H.L. Dreyfus and M.A. Wrathall (eds.), *A Companion to Heidegger* (pp. 49–64). Oxford: Blackwell, 2005.

Sara Heinämaa, Mirja Hartimo, and Timo Miettinen (eds.), *Phenomenology and the Transcendental*. London: Routledge, 2014.

William J. Lenkowski, "What is Husserl's epoche? The problem of beginning of philosophy in a Husserlian context." *Man and World* 11(3–4), 1978, 299–323.

4

SCIENCE AND THE LIFEWORLD

For many phenomenologists, the task of phenomenology is not to describe empirical and factual particularities, but to investigate the essential structures characterising our experiences, their correlates, and the connection between the two. As philosophers, our concern is not primarily with accidental features and properties, but with necessary and invariant ones. We are not concerned with the difference between the perception of a dime and a penny, or the difference between the desire for red wine and white wine; rather, our concern is with what characterises perception or desire in general. The perception of the dime and the perception of the penny differ in some respects, but they also have something in common, namely that which makes both acts perceptual acts rather than acts of imagination or recollection, and those features are what our analysis should aim to disclose. But how do we do that? How can we obtain insights into the essential structures of a given domain?

Before providing an answer, let me just emphasise that our ability to discriminate accidental and contingent features from more essential and necessary ones is an ability that is not only central to philosophy and science, but also one that we constantly and unproblematically employ in daily life. Consider, for example, the task of buying a new toothbrush. When standing in the pharmacy and looking at the

DOI: 10.4324/9781003350682-6

diverse models on offer, we immediately recognise them as being different types of toothbrushes, even if they differ somewhat in colour and size. We see variations in colour as being accidental to that which makes a toothbrush a toothbrush. Likewise, when looking for a specific book, I do not have a problem re-identifying it, even if somebody moved it, and it is now located at a different point in space than before. I immediately recognise that its spatial location is accidental to its identity, and that it does not change nature simply by being moved.

ESSENTIALISM

One of the tools employed by Husserl in his search for essential structures is what is known as the *eidetic variation* or *eidetic reduction*. The basic idea here is to take our point of departure in what is given to us, and then to use our imagination. By varying that which we are investigating, by imagining it as being different from how it actually is, we can slowly strip away its accidental properties, and thereby reach certain properties or features that cannot be changed without the object of investigation thereby also ceasing to be the kind of object it is. If we again consider the book, I might change the colour and design of the cover; I can add or subtract its number of pages; I can change its size and weight, etc. In performing this exercise, I am relying on both my previous experience of books and on the power of my imagination. The end result is the delimitation of a certain set of properties that belong to the book as such, and which, if changed, would make the book cease being a book. The imaginative variation can, consequently, help us disclose the invariant structures that make up the essence of the object.[1]

Although Husserl sometimes talks of the process in question as one that will result in a kind of eidetic or essential intuition (*Wesensschau*), it is important not to misunderstand his claims. First of all, Husserl is not suggesting that phenomenologists have access to some mysterious and infallible source of insight. The eidetic variation can be seen as a kind of imaginatively guided or aided conceptual analysis and has a quite different aim than empirical or experimental work, which it cannot replace. It is a demanding and open-ended process, and the results are in most cases defeasible. There is, in short, no claim to infallibility. Rather, the insights always possess a certain provisionality, a certain presumptiveness, and necessarily remain open for future modifications in the light of new evidence.[2] Secondly, Husserl sometimes distinguishes what he calls *exact essences* from *morphological essences*.[3] Whereas we in pure mathematics and other exact sciences are able to define matters with great precision, most of the entities studied by the human and social sciences are characterised by an essential vagueness, they possess morphological essences, and our classification and description of these entities are, by nature, approximative. To seek to impose the same exactness and precision that we find in geometry to matters in the world of everyday life is to do violence to the latter. Finally, when it comes to the task of phenomenology, Husserl certainly didn't see it as being concerned with disclosing the alleged essential structure of, say, marriages, elections, clarinets, or oak trees. Rather, Husserl was pursuing far more fundamental topics at a much higher level of generality. What are the general structures of intentionality, of embodiment, of temporality? What distinguishes perception from imagination? What characterises a physical object as such and how is it distinct from a mathematical entity or a psychological process?

It might be helpful to distinguish Husserl's commitment to the existence of invariant and universal structures from two alternative and quite opposed positions. On the one hand, Husserl's type of essentialism should not be conflated with the kind of (socio-biological) essentialism criticised by many scholars in racial, postcolonial, and feminist studies according to which race, ethnicity, gender, etc. are fixed, inherent, and ahistorical determinations. In such a view, being, say, a father, or a Dane, or a Jew is to possess certain fixed and unchanging properties that are common to all fathers, Danes, and Jews at all times. By contrast, as we shall also see in the following chapters, Husserl was well aware of how much notions like these are subject to historical and cultural changes.

On the other hand, Husserl's view must also be contrasted with the relativism espoused by some social constructivists. In their book *The Constructivist Credo*, Lincoln and Guba, for instance, argue that relativism is the basic ontological presupposition of constructivism, that objectivity is a chimera, and that the entities studied by the human sciences do not "really" exist, since they are purely conventional and only exist in the minds of the persons contemplating them.[4] To miss out on the crucial differences between a view like this and the position(s) espoused by Husserl and other phenomenologists would be a major mistake.

Given how widespread some form of essentialism has been in both science and (the history of) philosophy, it is important not to consider the reference to essential structures as distinctive of phenomenological philosophy. One should not equate the eidetic variation with the transcendental reduction. In fact, it would be a particularly egregious mistake to prioritise the former at the expense of the latter.

We have in earlier chapters seen how phenomenologists want to turn to the things themselves. The slogan indicates that our investigation should be critical and undogmatic and stay away from metaphysical speculations. It should be guided by what is actually given, rather than by what we expect to find given our theoretical commitments. Our method should be dictated by the subject matter at hand, rather than by veneration for a specific scientific ideal. As Heidegger remarks in *What is Metaphysics*, it is a mistake to equate scientific rigour with mathematical precision.[5] We should not simply assume that any domain that cannot be analysed with mathematical exactitude is less valuable or even less real.

Similar ideas can be found in Husserl, who, in the work *Formal and Transcendental Logic*, warns against the danger of letting oneself be dazzled by the methodology and ideals of the exact sciences, as if they constituted the absolute norms for what counts as true and real.[6] Rather than letting our predetermined theories decide what we can experience, we should let our theories be guided by the object of experience. We should let the phenomena speak:

> The true method follows the nature of the things to be investigated and not our prejudices and preconceptions.[7]
>
> What is needed is not the insistence that one see with his own eyes; rather it is that he not explain away under the pressure of prejudice what has been seen.[8]

As Husserl points out, the scientists might well employ more exact measurements than the market sellers, but this precision also has its own limitations. In fact, it is not of much use to the trader. If you want to sell a kilogram of oranges, you do not want to and do not need to measure the weight in micrograms. What is sufficient and appropriate and precise enough depends on the concrete context and cannot be defined in absolute terms.[9]

But are these maxims not uncontroversial trivialities? Not quite. In the phenomenological view, reality is complex and consists of a multitude of different ontological regions (be it the realm of idealities, of nature, of culture, etc.). Any investigation of these realms or regions should respect their peculiarities and distinct features and employ methods that are appropriate for the domain in question.[10] As a consequence, phenomenology has been outspoken in its criticism of a variety of different, partially overlapping, positions, including *reductionism*, *eliminativism*, and *naturalism*.

REDUCE OR ELIMINATE

Scientific reductionism is motivated by various methodological principles, including the one known as *Ockham's razor*. Do not assume the existence of more types of objects (or ontological realms) than is strictly necessary. If we are to choose between several theories, each of which treats its own part of reality, and a single theory, which in a systematic fashion can explain different parts of reality by reducing the more complex parts to less complex parts, we should choose the latter. This is not only because an increasing amount of unity, systematicity, and simplicity is theoretically satisfying, but also because the reduction in question is supposed to possess explanatory power. If a certain range of properties can be reduced to another range of properties, the former can be explained by the latter. A classic example is the attempt to explain an object's macro properties, such as temperature, transparency, solubility, or elasticity, by appeal to its micro properties, i.e., its molecular composition. A common assumption has, consequently, been that if we want an answer to the question "what is x?", then the question has to be reformulated as "how can x be reduced to something that can be understood by physics, chemistry or neurophysiology?" In addition, there is the assumption that unless such an answer can be given, unless the phenomenon under consideration can be reduced, it cannot be real. A formulation of this view can be found in Jerry

Fodor: "It's hard to see [. . .] how one can be a Realist about intentionality without also being, to some extent or other, a Reductionist. [. . .] If aboutness is real, it must be really something else".[11] The assumption has, consequently, been that only a reductive account of, say, consciousness can offer us a real insight into the nature of consciousness, and that consciousness will only be real if such a reductive account is possible.

The *eliminativist* shares many of the same concerns as the reductionist. Only that which can be accounted for using the methods and principles of the natural sciences count as real. But in contrast to the reductionist, the eliminativist argues that consciousness cannot be reduced to, say, neurophysiological processes. In her view, it is not possible to carry out this reduction. But rather than then drawing what would appear to be the natural conclusion – that consciousness is irreducible – she draws a different conclusion, namely that consciousness doesn't exist. For the eliminative materialist, our beliefs that there exists something like "desire, fear, sensation, joy, pain, and so on"[12] are nothing but theoretical assumptions that together constitute a primitive psychological theory. This primitive theory does not live up to the standards of contemporary science, it is not a credible psychological theory, and it therefore has to be rejected, just as one in the past has rejected, say, alchemy and phrenology. In short, the reason why it is impossible to reduce consciousness to respectable natural properties is because the former does not exist; consciousness is not real, but a fiction on a par with unicorns and yetis.

Scientific naturalism is distinguished by methodological as well as ontological commitments. The methodological commitment amounts to the idea that the correct procedures and the right types of justification are those found in and employed by the natural sciences. All genuine questions are natural scientific questions, and all genuine knowledge is knowledge gained by natural scientific means. To quote Galileo, whom Husserl sees as an early personification of this tendency:

Philosophy is written in this grand book, the universe, which stands continually open to our gaze. But the book cannot be understood unless one first learns to comprehend the language and read the letters in which it is composed. It is written in the language of mathematics, and its characters are triangles, circles, and other geometric figures without which it is humanly impossible to understand a single word of it; without these, one wanders about in a dark labyrinth.[13]

Historically speaking, considerations like these have often been coupled with ontological commitments according to which reality consists only of those entities, properties, and structures that are (or could be) accepted by natural science. Initially, the claim was that the form, size, and weight of an object, i.e., those features which can be described quantitatively with mathematical precision, are objective properties, whereas the colour, taste, and smell of the object are subjective phenomena that lack any mind-independent reality. This classical distinction between the primary and secondary qualities has over the years been radicalised and eventually led to the idea that it is not merely certain properties of the appearing object that lack objectivity, but everything that appears. The entire world of experience is a subjective construct, a wakeful dream, and if science is to disclose the true nature of reality, it consequently has to move beyond everything phenomenologically given. The world we live in, the world we are familiar with from experience, is quite different from the world of science, and only the latter deserves to be called real.

Jointly, the two commitments amount to the view that every truth is a natural scientific truth, and that everything which exists (including everything pertaining to human life, such as consciousness, intentionality, meaning, rationality, normativity, values, culture, history, etc.) must be studied by the methods of natural science and are ultimately explanatorily and ontologically reducible to natural scientific facts.

That we are dealing with radical positions should be obvious. If the shared slogan "reduce or eliminate" is true, many of the explanations found in the social and human sciences will be pseudo-explanations with no real scientific value. In addition, the reality of many of the objects and phenomena that are investigated by the social and human sciences will also be questionable. Consider phenomena such as money, stamps, symphonies, municipal elections, or wars. It is hard to see how it should be possible to account adequately for the currently ongoing wars in Ukraine or Gaza as political, cultural, social, and economic phenomena by means of the principles of neurophysiology, biology, or physics. But if the slogan is true, we would have to conclude that, strictly speaking, there never were any wars in Ukraine or Gaza. But is this not absurd, and does this kind of conclusion not present us with a *reductio ad absurdum* of the slogan?

THE LIFEWORLD

In the course of reflecting on the status of the world of science, phenomenologists have often emphasised the importance of the *lifeworld*. But what is the lifeworld, and what does it mean to claim that it has to be rehabilitated?

The lifeworld is, unsurprisingly, the world we live in. This is not a value-free world of quantifiable physical objects, chemical compounds, subatomic particles, or neural circuits. Rather, it is a world that contains tables, books, lamps, coffee cups, newspapers, trees, parks, roads, clouds, etc., i.e., more or less familiar objects of use and nature that we immediately relate to as interesting, accessible, extraneous, useless, etc. We are social beings and the world we inhabit is also populated by other people we meet as relatives, friends, colleagues, competitors, employees, strangers, etc. The lifeworld is the world we take for granted in daily life, it is the prescientific world of experience which we are all acquainted with, and which forms the basis of our daily actions and behaviour.

The world we primarily know and feel at home in is not a subject-independent reality, but a subject-relative world filled with human meaning. It is a world that is structured by references to our own bodily nature and location. We perceive things as affording actions – the cup affords drinking, the spoon eating, the chair sitting, the tree climbing – and as being to the left or right, as being within reach or further away, as accessible or inaccessible. It is also a historically and culturally shaped world, a world that constitutes the familiar horizon of meaning we as bodily subjects are anchored in and socialised into.

Why does this world need to be rehabilitated? Because the lifeworld has been forgotten and repressed by science, whose historical and systematic foundation it constitutes. Even the most exact and abstract scientific theories draw on the prescientific evidence of the lifeworld. In its search for objective knowledge, science has made a virtue of its ability to move beyond and surpass bodily, sensuous, and pragmatic experience, but has frequently overlooked to what extent it is enabled by those very same experiences. After all, it is often the perceived everyday object, and none other, that the "*physicist explores and scientifically determines following the method of physics*".[14] It is the planetary bodies observed in the sky, the water drunk, the flower admired, etc. that the natural scientist is also investigating and whose true nature she seeks to determine in as exact and objective a manner as possible. Even in those cases, however, where the object of the scientific investigation is far removed from everyday practice, the shared lifeworld remains in play, when planning and setting up the experiments, when reading the measuring instruments, when interpreting, comparing, and discussing the results with other scientists. Even though scientific theories in their precision and abstraction supersede the concrete and intuitively given lifeworld, the latter remains a constant source of reference.

It would be wrong to conceive of the relation between the lifeworld and the world of science as a static relation. Science draws on the lifeworld, but it also affects the lifeworld, and gradually its theoretical insights are absorbed by and integrated into the latter. Strasser has compared the lifeworld with fertile soil. Just as the soil might nourish a rich growth, the lifeworld can nourish theoretical knowledge. And just as the physical and chemical properties of the soil are modified by the plant growth it allows for, the lifeworld is modified and changed by the theoretical theories that it constitutes the foundation for.[15]

When phenomenologists highlight the significance of the lifeworld, this is not intended as a criticism of science. Phenomenology is not out to dispute the value of science and is not denying that scientific investigations can lead to new insights and expand our understanding of reality. But phenomenologists do reject the idea that natural science can provide an exhaustive account of reality. Importantly, this does not entail that phenomenology is, as such, opposed to quantitative methods and studies. The latter are excellent, but only when addressing quantitative questions. For phenomenology, the question of whether something is real or not, does not depend on whether it can fit the Procrustean bed of quantifiable science. Our world of experience has its own criteria of validity and truth and does not have to await the approval of science. Indeed, the findings of science and everyday experience do not have to contradict each other. They can both be true according to their own standards. More generally speaking, the difference between the world of experience and the world of science is for phenomenologists not a difference between the world for us and the world in itself, but a difference between two ways in which the world appears. The world of science is not an autonomous world, a world behind or below the manifest world. Rather, the world that science studies is the same world as that of everyday experience – namely, manifest reality – but now studied and explored in scientific terms. The world that can appear to us – be it in perception, in our daily concerns, or in our scientific analyses – is the only real world. To claim that in addition to this world there exists a world behind the scenes, which transcends every appearance and every experiential evidence, and to identify this world as the really real reality, is a move that is rejected by all phenomenologists.[16] Rather than defining objective reality as what is there *in itself*, rather than distinguishing how things are *for us* from how they are *simpliciter* in order then to insist that the investigation of the latter is the truly important one, we should face up to the fact that objectivity is an accomplishment that involves both subjectivity and intersubjectivity. Indeed, rather than being the antipode of objectivity, rather than constituting an obstacle and hindrance to scientific knowledge, (inter)subjectivity is for Husserl a necessary enabling condition. Husserl embraces a this-worldly conception of objectivity and reality and thereby dismisses the kind of scepticism that would argue that the way the world appears to us is compatible with the real world being completely different. Indeed, for Husserl, objectivity is precisely not defined in terms of mind-independence, but rather in relation to a community of minds. Objectivity is the outcome of an intersubjective process. It is what we can agree upon at the end of inquiry.

The view that only those entities and facts that are (or can be) known by natural science are objectively real does not only typically fail to properly engage with and address the philosophical question of what precisely reality and objectivity amount to. It is also a self-undermining enterprise in that it fails to adequately account for those experiential and cognitive achievements that make naturalism – as a specific attitude to and perspective on the world – possible in the first place.

Science often presents itself as an attempt to describe reality objectively, i.e., from a third-person perspective. The search for objectivity is, of course, laudable, but we shouldn't forget that any objectivity, any explanation, understanding, and theoretical modelling, presupposes first-person intentionality as its precondition. To that extent, the idea that science can deliver an absolute account of reality, one that is liberated from every theoretical and experiential perspective, is an illusion. Science is a distinct relation to the world, a particular theoretical modification of the natural attitude. This theoretical attitude did not fall down from the sky but has its own presuppositions and genesis. It is a tradition, a cultural formation. It is knowledge that is shared by a community of experiencing subjects and which presupposes a triangulation of points of view or perspectives. This is also why the usual opposition of first-person vs. third-person accounts is misleading. It makes us forget that third-person scientific accounts are accomplished and generated by a community of conscious subjects. There is no pure third-person perspective, just as there is no view from nowhere. This is, of course, not to say that there is no third-person perspective, but merely that such a perspective is, precisely, a perspective from somewhere. It is a view that *we* can adopt on the world. Science has its roots in the lifeworld, it draws on insights from the prescientific sphere, and is performed by embodied and embedded subjects. If we wish to comprehend the performance and limits of science, we must investigate the forms of intentionality that are employed by the cognising subjects. Without conscious subjects to interpret and discuss them, meter settings, computer printouts, x-ray pictures, and the like remain meaningless. Thus, according to this view, rather than being, as such, a hindrance or obstacle, consciousness turns out to be a far more important prerequisite for objectivity and the pursuit of scientific knowledge than, say, microscopes and telescopes. The aim of phenomenology is not to offer a competing scientific explanation of human beings, but to clarify our scientific practice, its rationality, and accomplishments, through a detailed analysis of the kinds of intentionality that the knowing subject(s) employ(s). How does the theoretical attitude that we employ when we conduct science arise out of and change our pre-theoretical being-in-the-world?

NOTES

1 Husserl, E. (1977). *Phenomenological Psychology: Lectures, Summer Semester, 1925*, trans. J. Scanlon. The Hague: Martinus Nijhoff: 53–65.
2 As a case in point, consider how the invention of digital books has led to a revised conception of what counts as a book.
3 Husserl, E. (1982). *Ideas Pertaining to a Pure Phenomenology and to a Phenomenological Philosophy. First Book. General Introduction to a Pure Phenomenology*, trans. F. Kersten. The Hague: Martinus Nijhoff: 164–167.
4 Lincoln, Y.S. and Guba, E.G. (2013). *The Constructivist Credo*. Walnut Creek, CA: Left Coast Press: 39–41.
5 Heidegger, M. (1993a). *Basic Writings*, ed. by D.F. Krell. San Francisco, CA: Harper: 94.
6 Husserl, E. (1969). *Formal and Transcendental Logic*, trans. D. Cairns. The Hague: Martinus Nijhoff: 278.
7 Husserl, E. (1965). Philosophy as rigorous science. In Q. Lauer (trans.), *Phenomenology and the Crisis of Philosophy* (pp. 71–147). New York, NY: Harper & Row: 102.
8 Husserl, E. (1965). Philosophy as rigorous science. In Q. Lauer (trans.), *Phenomenology and the Crisis of Philosophy* (pp. 71–147). New York, NY: Harper & Row: 147.
9 Husserl, E. (1969). *Formal and Transcendental Logic*, trans. D. Cairns. The Hague: Martinus Nijhoff: 278.
10 Heidegger, M. (1998). *Pathmarks*, ed. by W. McNeill. Cambridge: Cambridge University Press: 41.
11 Fodor, J. (1987). *Psychosemantics*. Cambridge, MA: MIT Press: 97.
12 Churchland, P.M. (1988). *Matter and Consciousness: A Contemporary Introduction to the Philosophy of Mind*. Revised edn. Cambridge, MA: MIT Press: 44.
13 Galileo, G. (1957). *Discoveries and Opinions of Galileo*. New York, NY: Anchor House: 237–238.
14 Husserl, E. (1982). *Ideas Pertaining to a Pure Phenomenology and to a Phenomenological Philosophy. First Book. General Introduction to a Pure Phenomenology*, trans. F. Kersten. The Hague: Martinus Nijhoff: 119.
15 Strasser, S. (1963). *Phenomenology and the Human Sciences: A Contribution to a New Scientific Ideal*. Pittsburgh, PA: Duquesne University Press: 71.
16 See, for instance, Husserl, E. (1982). *Ideas Pertaining to a Pure Phenomenology and to a Phenomenological Philosophy. First Book. General Introduction to a Pure Phenomenology*, trans. F. Kersten. The Hague: Martinus Nijhoff: 122.

SUGGESTIONS FOR FURTHER READING

Eran Dorfman, "History of the lifeworld: From Husserl to Merleau-Ponty." *Philosophy Today* 53(3), 2009, 294–303.

Robert Hanna, "Husserl's crisis and our crisis." *International Journal of Philosophical Studies* 22(5), 2014, 752–770.

Klaus Held, "Husserl's phenomenology of the life-world." In D. Welton (ed.), *The New Husserl: A Critical Reader* (pp. 32–62). Bloomington, IN: Indiana University Press, 2003.

Anthony Steinbock, *Home and Beyond: Generative Phenomenology after Husserl.* Evanston, IL: Northwestern University Press, 1995.

5

DIGGING DEEPER
From surface to depth phenomenology

One way to appraise the development of phenomenology is to see it as a continuous expansion, deepening, and complexification of the basic phenomenological analysis that we find in Husserl's early work. Husserl himself eventually came to label the kind of phenomenology he initially had conducted as a *static phenomenology*. If we consider some of the early formative analyses of perceptual intentionality and of the relation between perception and imagination, they all studied the intentional correlation with no regard for genesis and historicity. The type of object and the type of intentional act were both considered readily available. Subsequently, however, Husserl came to realise that the subject of intentionality is not merely a formal principle of constitution, it is not, as he puts it, "a dead pole of identity",[1] and the same holds true on the object side. Husserl went on to examine how patterns of understanding are gradually established and how they come to influence and enable subsequent experiences. Through a process of sedimentation, our experiences leave their trace in us and thereby contribute to the formation of cognitive schemas and diverse forms of apprehension and expectations that guide and motivate subsequent experiences. Certain types of intentionality (pre-linguistic experiences, for example) condition later and more complex types of intentionality (conceptual judgments, for instance), and

DOI: 10.4324/9781003350682-7

Husserl took the task of what he eventually called *genetic phenomenology* to involve the examination of the temporal becoming of these different forms of intentionality, one that also traced higher-order forms of objectivity back to lower-order forms.[2] The scope of genetic phenomenology remained restricted to the experiential life of an individual ego, however. In the last phase of his thinking, Husserl ventured into what has been called *generative phenomenology*.[3] The focus was broadened to investigate the constitutive role of tradition and history. In what way are the accomplishments of previous generations operative in our individual experiences? As Husserl would put it in a manuscript from the twenties, "everything of my own is founded, in part through the tradition of my ancestors, in part through the tradition of my contemporaries".[4]

GENERATIVITY AND TRADITION

One way this development is traced out in Husserl's own writings is through an increased focus on how the topics of embodiment, temporality, and sociality are intertwined. As we have already seen, Husserl argued that the body is essentially involved in the perception of and interaction with spatial objects. For him, the world is given to us as bodily explored, and the body is revealed to us in its exploration of the world. Early on, Husserl also came to realise the importance of temporality, and defended the view that an investigation of intentionality will remain incomplete as long as one ignores the temporal dimension of the intentional acts and intentional objects. In addition, Husserl was one of the first philosophers to employ and discuss the notion of intersubjectivity in a comprehensive and systematic manner. He worked on empathy for more than three decades and would eventually declare that phenomenology had to develop from an "'egological' phenomenology" to a "sociological phenomenology".[5]

In Husserl's last writings, the topics of embodiment, intersubjectivity, and temporality are brought and thought together. There is also a diachronic dimension to intersubjectivity. Ultimately, Husserl would consider the subject's birth into a living tradition to have constitutive implications. It is not merely the case that I live in a world which is permeated by references to others, and which others have already furnished with meaning, or that I understand the world (and myself) through a traditional, handed-down, linguistic conventionality. The very meaning that the world has for me is such that it has its origin outside of me, in a historical past. As Husserl writes in *Crisis*, being embedded in "the unitary flow of a historical development" – in a generative nexus of birth and death – belongs as indissolubly to the I as does its temporal form.[6]

The fact that Husserl eventually came to include topics such as embodiment, historicity, and intersubjectivity in his transcendental analysis is one of the reasons why Merleau-Ponty in the preface to *Phenomenology of Perception* could write: "Husserl's transcendental is not Kant's".[7]

Husserl's late ideas regarding the intertwinement between self, others, and world is, from early on, also pursued by Heidegger and Merleau-Ponty, who likewise insist that self, world, and others belong together; that they reciprocally illuminate one another and can only be understood in their interconnection. In an early lecture, Heidegger describes the lifeworld as an interpenetration of the three domains: surrounding world, with-world, and self-world,[8] and argues that Dasein as world-experiencing is always already being-with (*Mitsein*) others. As he would put it in later lectures from 1927:

Dasein is just as little at first merely a dwelling among things so as then occasionally to discover among these things beings with its own kind of being; instead, as the being which is occupied with itself, the Dasein is with equal originality being-with others *and* being-among intraworldly beings.[9]

As for Merleau-Ponty, he argues that subjectivity is essentially oriented and open toward that which it is not, and that it is in this openness that it reveals itself to itself. What is disclosed by a phenomenological reflection is, consequently, not a self-enclosed mind, a pure interior self-presence, but an openness toward otherness, a movement of exteriorisation and perpetual self-transcendence. It is by being present to the world that we are present to ourselves, and it is by being given to ourselves that we can be conscious of the world.[10] Merleau-Ponty consequently insists that a phenomenological description, rather than disclosing subjectivities that are inaccessible and self-sufficient, reveals continuities between inter-subjective life and the world. The subject is present to itself, to the world, and to others, not in spite of, but precisely by way of its corporeality and historicity.[11] As Merleau-Ponty fully realises, such a conception of the intertwinement of self, others, and world affects the very conception of transcendental philosophy:

> [H]ow can the borders of the transcendental and the empirical help becoming indistinct? For along with the other person, all the other person sees of me – all my facticity – is reintegrated into subjectivity, or at least posited as an indispensable element of its definition. Thus the transcendental descends into history. Or as we might put it, the historical is no longer an external relation between two or more absolutely autonomous subjects but has an interior and is an inherent aspect of their very definition. They no longer know themselves to be subjects simply in relation to their individual selves, but in relation to one another as well.[12]

How does the phenomenological work of Merleau-Ponty and Heidegger diverge from that of Husserl? One way to conceive of the divergence is by seeing both as pursuing ideas already found in Husserl in a more radical manner than Husserl himself.

Merleau-Ponty attributes more significance to the role of embodiment and facticity, i.e., the contingent situatedness of our existence, than Husserl, and also goes further in his attempt to rethink the traditional divide between the transcendental and the empirical and between mind and world. Merleau-Ponty was far more concerned with discussions in contemporary psychology and neurology than Husserl had been, and this interest also left its mark on his writings. Merleau-Ponty's first major work, *The Structure of Behavior* (1942), engages extensively with empirical science and on its final page Merleau-Ponty calls for a redefinition of transcendental philosophy.[13] Rather than making us choose between a scientific explanation and a phenomenological reflection, Merleau-Ponty asks us to respect the living relation between consciousness and nature and to search for a dimension that is beyond both objectivism and subjectivism. This approach is further pursued in *Phenomenology of Perception* (1945), where Merleau-Ponty, for instance, discusses studies by the neurologist Kurt Goldstein and the neuropsychologist Adhémar Gelb of the brain-damaged patient Johann Schneider.

Heidegger is a more attentive reader of the history of philosophy than Husserl and is also, to a larger extent than Husserl, highlighting the extent to which our current thinking is influenced by the tradition. For Heidegger, one important task of phenomenology is to disclose and deconstruct some of the metaphysical conceptions that for centuries have tacitly framed and constrained philosophical thinking. In the course of his own phenomenological analysis, Heidegger came to question the traditional privileging of the theoretical attitude, of object-givenness, and of temporal presence. He argues that one of Husserl's limitations was that he remained too focused on logical and epistemological issues and thereby operated with too narrow a concept of being and givenness. Rather than letting his investigation be guided by the things themselves, Husserl was, according to Heidegger, instead led by traditional, or to be more specific, by Cartesian presuppositions and decisions. By privileging the active ego, and by reducing givenness to object-givenness, Husserl not only failed to disclose the unique mode of being peculiar to intentional subjectivity, he also failed to engage adequately with the truly transcendental question concerning the condition of possibility for givenness as such.[14] In works succeeding *Being and Time*, Heidegger's own wrestling with these issues led him to question his own prior privileging of Dasein. Whereas in *Being and Time*, he still argued that a fundamental ontology must be rooted in human existence and that we have to approach the ontological questions via an investigation of Dasein's understanding of being, Heidegger subsequently came to hold the view that Dasein's own understanding is enabled by a more fundamental clearing (*Lichtung*) that belongs to being itself. As Heidegger writes in *Letter on "Humanism"* from 1946:

> The human being is not the lord of beings. The human being is the shepherd of being. Human beings lose nothing in this "less"; rather, they gain in that they attain the truth of being. They gain the essential poverty of the shepherd, whose dignity consists in being called by being itself into the preservation of being's truth.[15]

So far, I have primarily been characterising the development of phenomenology as an expansion of focus. One might, however, also describe the development in a somewhat different, more vertical, manner.

PHENOMENOLOGY OF THE INVISIBLE

It has become customary to distinguish *surface phenomenology* from *depth phenomenology*. Whereas the former focuses squarely on the correlation between specific types of objects and specific intentional acts, it is also possible to proceed in a more radical manner. Sometimes, Husserl speaks of the need for an elaborate *mining effort* if one is to uncover and disclose how the intentional activity of the subject is founded upon and conditioned by various processes of passivity taking place in the underground or depth-dimension of subjectivity.[16] Husserl was well aware of the fact that any description of this passive and anonymously functioning dimension is beset with difficulties, mainly because the concepts we have at our disposal primarily originate from our interaction with worldly objects. One challenge is, consequently, to avoid importing too clear distinctions and overly objectifying structures and categories into our description of experiential life. Realising these difficulties, Husserl at one point emphasised that the most fundamental dimension of subjectivity "lies almost at the limit of possible description".[17]

More generally speaking, Husserl fully recognised that object-intentionality, our consciousness of and preoccupation with objects, doesn't exhaust the life of the mind and, indeed, has various preconditions of its own. Husserl's investigation into the structures of time-consciousness is often viewed as his most radical attempt at characterising and analysing the most fundamental phenomenological dimension. One noteworthy feature of Husserl's extensive engagement with time-consciousness is precisely that he eventually came to realise that there are other forms of manifestation than object-manifestation (thereby also questioning the accuracy of Heidegger's criticism), and that the temporal self-manifestation of consciousness is subjected to very different principles and structures than the manifestation of chairs and tables.

In a famous remark in *Being and Time*, Heidegger observes that the specific task of phenomenology is to disclose that which first and foremost remains hidden from view. Indeed, it is exactly because there are phenomena that do not reveal themselves immediately that we are in need of a phenomenology.[18] Much later, in a conference from 1973, Heidegger explicitly spoke of the need for a "phenomenology of the inapparent".[19] The perhaps most sustained attempt to push the boundaries of phenomenology in this direction can be found in the work of Michel Henry who sought to develop what has been called a *phenomenology of the invisible*. Briefly put, Henry's idea was that subjectivity does not reveal itself in the light of the world, in the visibility of worldly exteriority. Pure subjectivity does not reveal itself as a worldly object and cannot be captured through categories pertaining to worldly appearance. Rather, as Henry writes:

> The foundation is not something obscure, neither is it light which becomes perceivable only when it shines upon the thing which bathes in its light, nor is it the thing itself as a "transcendent phenomenon", but it is an *immanent* revelation which is a presence to itself, even though such a presence remains "invisible".[20]

Henry's suggestion is not that phenomenology should abandon its interest in manifestation and instead engage in unconstrained speculations. To speak of the invisible is, for him, not to speak of something that forever remains hidden, it is not to speak of something that never manifests itself, but simply to speak of something that manifests itself in a radically different manner than the visible.

The idea that phenomenology has to move beyond an occupation and fixation with object-intentionality and object-manifestation is shared by most phenomenologists. This is so, not only because our most fundamental self-acquaintance does not take the form of an object-relation, and because our most fundamental relation to the world is not a relation to an object or complex of objects, but also because our authentic relationship to another subject is precisely a relation to someone that transcends our objectifying grasp.

Although these ideas can already be found in rudimentary form in Husserl, there is no question that later thinkers like Emmanuel

Levinas, Michel Henry, and Jacques Derrida, through their critical engagement with the classical phenomenological investigations of intentionality, time-consciousness, intersubjectivity, language, etc., radicalised the effort to disclose new types of manifestation, and thereby also made important contributions to the development of phenomenology.

NOTES

1 Husserl, E. (1977). *Phenomenological Psychology: Lectures, Summer Semester, 1925*, trans. J. Scanlon. The Hague: Martinus Nijhoff: 159.

2 Husserl, E. (2001a). *Die "Bernauer Manuskripte" über das Zeitbewußtsein (1917/18)*, ed. by R. Bernet and D. Lohmar. Husserliana 33. Dordrecht: Kluwer Academic Publishers: 634.

3 Steinbock, A.J. (1995). *Home and Beyond: Generative Phenomenology after Husserl*. Evanston, IL: Northwestern University Press.

4 Husserl, E. (1973a). *Zur Phänomenologie der Intersubjektivität II. Texte aus dem Nachlass. Zweiter Teil. 1921–1928*, ed. by I. Kern. Husserliana 14. The Hague: Martinus Nijhoff: 223.

5 Husserl, E. (1981). *Shorter Works*, ed. by P. McCormick and F.A. Elliston. Notre Dame, IN: University of Notre Dame Press: 68.

6 Husserl, E. (1970). *The Crisis of European Sciences and Transcendental Phenomenology: An Introduction to Phenomenological Philosophy*, trans. D. Carr. Evanston, IL: Northwestern University Press: 253.

7 Merleau-Ponty, M. (2012). *Phenomenology of Perception*, trans. D.A. Landes. London: Routledge: lxxvii.

8 Heidegger, M. (1993b). *Grundprobleme der Phänomenologie (1919/1920)*. Gesamtausgabe Band 58. Frankfurt am Main: Vittorio Klostermann: 33, 39, 62.

9 Heidegger, M. (1982). *The Basic Problems of Phenomenology*, trans. A. Hofstadter. Bloomington, IN: Indiana University Press: 297.

10 Merleau-Ponty, M. (2012). *Phenomenology of Perception*, trans. D.A. Landes. London: Routledge: 311, 396, 448.

11 Merleau-Ponty, M. (2012). *Phenomenology of Perception*, trans. D.A. Landes. London: Routledge: 478.

12 Merleau-Ponty, M. (1964a). *Signs*, trans. R.C. McClearly. Evanston, IL: Northwestern University Press: 107.

13 Merleau-Ponty, M. (1963). *The Structure of Behavior*, trans. A.L. Fisher. Boston, MA: Beacon Press: 224.

14 Heidegger, M. (1985). *History of the Concept of Time: Prolegomena*, trans. T. Kisiel. Bloomington, IN: Indiana University Press: §§ 10–13.

15 Heidegger, M. (1998). *Pathmarks*, ed. by W. McNeill. Cambridge: Cambridge University Press: 260.

16 Husserl, E. (2001a). *Die "Bernauer Manuskripte" über das Zeitbewußtsein (1917/18)*, ed. by R. Bernet and D. Lohmar. Husserliana 33. Dordrecht: Kluwer Academic Publishers: 170.
17 Husserl, E. (2001c). *Analyses Concerning Passive and Active Synthesis: Lectures on Transcendental Logic*, trans. A. Steinbock. Dordrecht: Kluwer Academic Publishers: 278.
18 Heidegger, M. (1996). *Being and Time*, trans. J. Stambaugh. Albany, NY: SUNY: 31.
19 Heidegger, M. (2003). *Four Seminars*, trans. A. Mitchell and F. Raffoul. Bloomington, IN: Indiana University Press: 80.
20 Henry, M. (1973). *The Essence of Manifestation*, trans. G. Etzkorn. The Hague: Martinus Nijhoff: 41.

SUGGESTIONS FOR FURTHER READING

Françoise Dastur, "French phenomenology after 1961." In M. Sinclair and D. Whistler (eds.), *The Oxford Handbook of Modern French Philosophy* (pp. 319–333). Oxford: Oxford University Press, 2024.

Jacques Derrida, "Violence and metaphysics: An essay on the thought of Emmanuel Levinas." In J. Derrida, *Writing and Difference*, trans. Alan Bass (pp. 79–153). London: Routledge, 1995.

Martin C. Dillon, "Merleau-Ponty and the reversibility thesis." *Man and World* 16(4), 1983, 365–388.

Dan Zahavi, "Michel Henry and the phenomenology of the invisible." *Continental Philosophy Review* 32(3), 1999, 223–240.

6

MERLEAU-PONTY'S PREFACE TO *PHENOMENOLOGY OF PERCEPTION*

Let me conclude Part I by looking at the famous preface that Merleau-Ponty wrote to his most well-known work, *Phenomenology of Perception*. The preface seeks to give a short answer to the question "What is phenomenology?" Since Merleau-Ponty, in his discussion, draws on insights from both Husserl and Heidegger, the preface is a suitable candidate for a nuanced reply.

As Merleau-Ponty starts out by observing, even half a century after Husserl's first writings a univocal definition of phenomenology is still missing. In fact, many of the proposals given seem to point in different directions:

1 On the one hand, phenomenology is characterised by a form of essentialism. It is not interested in a merely empirical or factual account of different phenomena, but seeks, on the contrary, to disclose the invariant structures of, for example, the stream of consciousness, embodiment, perception, etc. On the other hand, however, the point of departure for its investigation of the world and human existence remains factual existence. Phenomenology is not simply a form of essentialism, it is also a philosophy of facticity.
2 Phenomenology is a form of transcendental philosophy. It seeks to disclose the conditions of possibility of intentional experience

DOI: 10.4324/9781003350682-8

and worldly objectivity, and it suspends our natural and everyday metaphysical assumptions (in particular, our assumption about the existence of a mind-independent world) in order to investigate them critically. At the same time, however, it concedes that reflection must start from an already existing relation to the world, and that a central task of philosophy is to comprehend this immediate and direct contact with the world.

3 Phenomenology seeks to establish a strictly scientific philosophy, but it also has the task of accounting for our lifeworld and of doing justice to our pre-scientific experience of space, time, and world.

4 Phenomenology is frequently described as a purely descriptive discipline. It describes our experiences just as they are given. It is interested neither in the neurophysiological nor the biological origins of the experiences, nor does it seek to provide a causal account. But at the same time, Husserl himself had emphasised the importance of developing a genetic phenomenology, i.e., a phenomenology that analyses the origin, development, and historicity of the intentional structures.

As Merleau-Ponty remarks, it might be tempting to seek to overcome these apparent discrepancies by simply differentiating between Husserl's (transcendental) phenomenology, which has often been seen as an attempt to thematise the pure and invariant conditions of cognition, and Heidegger's (hermeneutical and existential) phenomenology, which has frequently been interpreted as an attempt to disclose the historical and practical contextuality of our being-in-the-world. But Merleau-Ponty quickly rejects this suggestion as being too naive. As he points out, all the contrasts mentioned can be found internally in Husserl's thinking. Moreover, and more importantly, we are not dealing with true contrasts or alternatives, but rather with complementary aspects that phenomenology (if properly understood) necessarily includes and incorporates.[1]

Husserl's dictum "to the things themselves" is interpreted by Merleau-Ponty as a criticism of scientism, and as an attempt to disclose a more original relation to the world than the one manifested in scientific rationality. It is a call for a return to the world of perceptual experience that is prior to and more fundamental than the world of scientific conceptualisation and articulation. Scientism seeks to reduce us to objects in the world, objects that can be exhaustively explained by objectifying theories like those of physics, biology, or psychology. It argues that the methods of natural science provide the sole means of epistemic access to the world, and that entities that cannot be captured in terms accepted by natural science are non-existent. As Merleau-Ponty insists, however, we should never forget that our knowledge of the world, including our scientific knowledge, arises from a bodily anchored first-person perspective, and that science would be meaningless without this experiential dimension. The scientific discourse is rooted in the world of experience, in the experiential world, and if we wish to comprehend the performance and limits of science, we should investigate the original experience of the world of which science is a higher-order articulation. The one-sided focus of science on what is available from a third-person perspective is, for Merleau-Ponty, consequently both naive and dishonest, since the scientific practice constantly presupposes the scientist's first-personal and pre-scientific experience of the world.[2]

Phenomenology's highlighting of the importance of the first-person perspective should not be conflated with the classical (transcendental) idealistic attempt to detach the mind from the world in order to let a pure and worldless subject constitute the richness and concreteness of the world. This attempt was also naive. The subject has no priority over the world, and truth is not to be found in the interiority of man. There is no interiority, since man is in the world, and only knows him- or herself by means of inhabiting the world. To put it differently, the subjectivity disclosed by the phenomenological reflection is not a concealed interiority, but an open world-relation.[3] To use Heidegger's phrase, we are precisely dealing with a being-in-the-world, a world that moreover should not be understood as the mere totality of objects, or as the sum total of causal relations, but rather as the context of meaning that we are constantly situated within.

Had idealism been true, had the world been a mere product of our constitution and construction, the world would have appeared in full transparency. It would only possess the meaning that we ascribed to it and would consequently contain no hidden aspects, no sense of mystery. Idealism and constructivism deprive the world of its transcendence. For such positions, knowledge of self, world, and other are no longer a problem. But things are more complicated.

As a careful phenomenological analysis will reveal, I do not simply exist for myself, but also for others, just as others do not simply exist for themselves, but also for me. The subject does not have a monopoly, either on its self-understanding or on its understanding of the world. On the contrary, there are aspects of myself and aspects of the world that only become available and accessible through the other. In short, my existence is not simply a question of how I apprehend myself, it is also a question of how others apprehend me. Subjectivity is necessarily embedded and embodied in a social, historical, and natural context. The world is inseparable from subjectivity and intersubjectivity, and the task of phenomenology is to think world, subjectivity, and intersubjectivity in their proper connection.[4]

Our relation to the world is so fundamental, so obvious and natural, that we normally do not reflect upon it. It is this domain of ignored obviousness that phenomenology seeks to investigate. The task of phenomenology is not to obtain new empirical knowledge about different areas in the world, but rather to comprehend the basic relation to the world that is presupposed by any such empirical investigation. When phenomenology emphasises the methodological necessity of a type of reflective restraint – what Husserl has called the epoché and reduction – this is not because phenomenology intends to desert the world in favour of pure consciousness, but because we can only make those intentional threads that attach us to the world visible by slacking them slightly. The world is, as Merleau-Ponty writes, wonderful. It is a gift and a riddle. But in order to realise this, it is necessary to suspend our ordinary blind and thoughtless taking of the world for granted. Normally, I live in a natural and engaged world-relation. But as a philosopher, I cannot make do with such a naive world-immersion. I must distance myself from it, if ever so slightly, in order to be able to account for it. This is why Merleau-Ponty argues that an analysis of our being-in-the-world presupposes the phenomenological reduction.[5]

The phenomenological investigation proceeds from the factual to the essential, but that is not where the analysis ends. The focus on the essential is not the goal, but a means to understand, conceptualise, and articulate the depth of our factual existence. The focus on essential structures is due to a wish to capture the richness of the factual, and not because of a desire to abstract from and ignore facticity.[6]

The analysis of intentionality, the analysis of the directedness or aboutness of consciousness, is often presented as one of the central accomplishments of phenomenology. One does not merely love, fear, see, or judge, one loves a beloved, fears something fearful, sees an object, and judges a state of affairs. Regardless of whether we are talking about a perception, thought, judgment, fantasy, doubt, expectation, or recollection, all of these diverse forms of consciousness are characterised by intending objects and cannot be analysed properly without a look at their objective correlate, e.g., the perceived, doubted, or expected object. It is, consequently, not a problem for the subject to reach the object, since its being is intentional. That is, the subject is per se self-transcending, per se directed towards something different from itself. But apart from having analysed our theoretical object-directedness in great detail, phenomenology has also made it clear that the world is given prior to any analysis, identification, and objectification. There is, in short, also a pre- and a-theoretical relation to the world. As Merleau-Ponty points out, this is why Husserl distinguished two types of intentionality. There is what Husserl in *Logical Investigations* called *act-intentionality*, which is an objectifying form of intentionality. But there is also a more fundamental passive or *operative* form of non-objectifying intentionality, which Husserl analysed in detail in some of his later works. According to Merleau-Ponty, this original and basic world-relation cannot be explained or analysed further. All phenomenology can do is to call attention to it and make us respect its irreducibility.[7]

Merleau-Ponty characterises phenomenology as a perpetual critical (self-)reflection. It should not take anything for granted, least of all itself. It is, to put it differently, a constant meditation.[8] Merleau-Ponty's point here is that phenomenology is always *en route*. This also comes to the fore in Merleau-Ponty's famous assertion that "the most important lesson of the reduction is the impossibility of a complete reduction".[9] The reduction must be seen as a particular reflective move, and Merleau-Ponty's point is that we as finite creatures are incapable of effectuating an absolute reflection that once and for all would allow us to cut our ties to our world-immersed life in order to survey it from a view from nowhere. Even the most radical reflection depends upon and is linked to an unreflected life that, as Merleau-Ponty puts it, remains its initial, constant, and final situation.[10] To say that the reduction cannot be completed is not to say that it cannot be carried out. But this procedure is something that has to be performed repeatedly, rather than completed once and for all. To that extent, Merleau-Ponty's remarks about the unfinished character of phenomenology and about the incomplete reduction are two ways of making the same point. As Merleau-Ponty points out in closing, however, the fact that phenomenology remains unfinished, the fact that it is always under way, is not a defect or flaw that should be mended, but rather one of its essential features. As a wonder over the world, phenomenology is not a solid and inflexible system, but rather in constant movement.[11]

NOTES

1 Merleau-Ponty, M. (2012). *Phenomenology of Perception*, trans. D.A. Landes. London: Routledge: lxxi.
2 Merleau-Ponty, M. (2012). *Phenomenology of Perception*, trans. D.A. Landes. London: Routledge: lxxii.
3 Merleau-Ponty, M. (2012). *Phenomenology of Perception*, trans. D.A. Landes. London: Routledge: lxxiv.
4 Merleau-Ponty, M. (2012). *Phenomenology of Perception*, trans. D.A. Landes. London: Routledge: lxxvi, lxxxv.
5 Merleau-Ponty, M. (2012). *Phenomenology of Perception*, trans. D.A. Landes. London: Routledge: lxxviii.
6 Merleau-Ponty, M. (2012). *Phenomenology of Perception*, trans. D.A. Landes. London: Routledge: lxxviii.
7 Merleau-Ponty, M. (2012). *Phenomenology of Perception*, trans. D.A. Landes. London: Routledge: lxxxii.
8 Merleau-Ponty, M. (2012). *Phenomenology of Perception*, trans. D.A. Landes. London: Routledge: lxxxv.
9 Merleau-Ponty, M. (2012). *Phenomenology of Perception*, trans. D.A. Landes. London: Routledge: lxxvii.
10 Merleau-Ponty, M. (2012). *Phenomenology of Perception*, trans. D.A. Landes. London: Routledge: lxxviii.
11 Merleau-Ponty, M. (2012). *Phenomenology of Perception*, trans. D.A. Landes. London: Routledge: xvi.

SUGGESTIONS FOR FURTHER READING

Martin C. Dillon, *Merleau-Ponty's Ontology*. 2nd edn. Evanston, IL: Northwestern University Press, 1997.

Komarine Romdenh-Romluc, *Merleau-Ponty and Phenomenology of Perception*. London: Routledge, 2010.

Ted Toadvine, "Maurice Merleau-Ponty." In E.N. Zalta and U. Nodelman (eds.), *The Stanford Encyclopedia of Philosophy*, 2023: https://plato.stanford.edu/archives/win2023/entries/merleau-ponty/.

PART II

CONCRETE ANALYSES

After having characterised the nature of phenomenological philosophy and discussed a number of fundamental phenomenological concepts and distinctions, it is now time to see phenomenology at work. Phenomenology is rightly renowned for its meticulous investigations, and in the following I will exemplify this richness by considering some concrete phenomenological analyses. I will first examine phenomenological explorations of spatiality and embodiment, then turn to analyses of intersubjectivity and community, and finally discuss what has become known as critical phenomenology.

DOI: 10.4324/9781003350682-9

7

SPATIALITY AND EMBODIMENT

One of Heidegger's influential claims in *Being and Time* is that the philosophical tradition has been too preoccupied and concerned with a specific kind of being, namely the being of objects. As a result, it has also tended to view human beings, i.e., the kind of beings that we ourselves are, as objects. This might at first seem like a strange claim; after all, has early modern philosophy including Descartes, Locke, and Hume not precisely been highlighting the importance of subjectivity? According to Heidegger, however, there has been a widespread tendency to conceive of subjectivity as a self-contained and worldless substance, i.e., as a very special kind of isolated object. Such an approach has, however, utterly failed to do justice to our own distinctive mode of being. We are first and foremost beings constituted by our relationship to the very world that we inhabit.

BEING-IN-THE-WORLD

To mark the rupture with traditional conceptions, Heidegger introduced the term *Dasein* to designate the kind of beings we ourselves are, and most of *Being and Time* is devoted to an analysis of its fundamental features, in particular its so-called being-in-the-world

DOI: 10.4324/9781003350682-10

(*In-der-Welt-sein*). As Heidegger points out, we need to distinguish sharply between the *existential* "Being-in" of Dasein and the *categorial* "being in" of things. Dasein is not in the world in the same way as a t-shirt is in a closet – that is to say, as one extended entity being contained within another extended entity. In fact, given that Heidegger defines the world, not as an empty space or as the sum total of all objects, but rather as the context of meaning and significance that Dasein inhabits, it is no wonder that only Dasein, according to Heidegger, is characterised by being-in-the-world. Other types of entities, by contrast, are "innerworldly" or "belong to the world", but the world is not "there" for them, they have no world.[1]

For Heidegger, worldly engagement is a constitutive feature of Dasein, i.e., an essential feature that Dasein cannot lack. Moreover, this engagement does not primarily take the form of a detached theoretical observation and contemplation of detached objects, of what Heidegger terms the *present-at-hand*. Rather, the kind of entities we first and foremost encounter are entities that are *ready-to-hand*, entities that we can grab, manipulate, and use. Indeed, it is in practical use, it is by handling, using, and taking care of things, that they show themselves as what they are. As Heidegger writes:

> The less we just stare at the thing called hammer, the more actively we use it, the more original our relation to it becomes and the more undisguisedly it is encountered as what it is, as a useful thing. The act of hammering itself discovers the specific "handiness" of the hammer.[2]

More generally speaking, it is not cognition (here understood narrowly as a theoretical scrutiny of objects) that establishes the relation between Dasein and world. Rather, in cognition, Dasein established a new kind of relationship to entities in an already disclosed world. Cognition is a derived modification of our primary being-in-the-world and is only possible because we already are in the world. It is only because of our practical engagement with the ready-to-hand that something like a theoretical exploration of such entities becomes possible. It is only because we use the vacuum cleaner that circumstances can occur where that use is disturbed, say, if the vacuum cleaner ceases to work properly, and it is precisely then that, rather than being absorbed in the job at hand, we start to notice and scrutinise the utensil itself as a present-at-hand object that possesses extension, weight, colour, etc.[3]

In section 22 of *Being and Time*, Heidegger raises the question regarding the spatiality of innerworldly entities. Not surprisingly, he is at first interested in the spatiality of the ready-to-hand, since his point of departure is the kind of entities that we first and foremost encounter. As Heidegger points out, the expression "first and foremost" does not merely have a temporal, but also a spatial connotation. Space is in the first instance a feature of the ready-to-hand, and not an empty container which can subsequently be filled with objects. It is only when our practical dealings are disturbed that we notice mere space; it is only when the flashlight is not where we expected to find it that we notice the drawer as an empty container.

That which we first and foremost encounter is that which is nearby. Given Heidegger's rejection of the primacy of the present-at-hand, nearness is not to be interpreted in geometrical terms. The ready-to-hand is nearby if it is *accessible* and *usable*. More specifically, the spatiality of the ready-to-hand, its place, is a matter of its embeddedness in a specific context of use, where it belongs and has its functionality, and not a matter of its location in three-dimensional space. It is only within such a pragmatic context that the utensil has significance, relevance, and usability. Single pieces of equipment never stand alone, but are always enmeshed in a network of references to other pieces of equipment. A stamp is only meaningful in a world that contains envelopes or postcards; a pen is for writing and refers to ink and paper; a hammer is a hammer only in the context of other equipment such as nails and boards. When we ask *where* something is, our question concerns its location within such a network. The spatial dimensions – above, beneath, next to, etc. – have such practical and concrete references. Distance cannot be defined in absolute terms, but is relative to context, practical concerns, and interests. Likewise, that which is closest by is not necessarily that which is at the shortest "objective" distance from one's own body. Rather, it is that which Dasein is concerned with, can reach out for, catch hold of, or see. To bring something closer is to incorporate it in the context of concernful dealings and use. To give a few concrete examples:

- Whereas geometrically, I am closer to the ground on which I am standing, or the spectacles I am wearing, than to the painting I am looking at, a phenomenological description will claim that I am closer to the painting than to the ground or my spectacles.[4]
- Geometrically, the distance between Copenhagen and New Delhi is pretty much the same as it was 100 years ago. Pragmatically, however, the distance has been reduced dramatically – at least for those of us who can afford the flight.
- When choosing one of two ways to achieve a certain goal, it is not always the geometrically shortest way that is pragmatically closest to the goal. If you have forgotten to bring your keys, and you are standing outside your locked front door, the geometrical proximity of the entrance hall does not prevent it from being pragmatically out of reach and, hence, remote. The moment you turn away from the front door and head for the unlocked back door, you are moving away from the entrance hall in geometrical terms, but moving closer in pragmatic terms: "The objective distances of objectively present things do not coincide with the remoteness and nearness of what is at hand within the world".[5]
- A town that is 10 miles away may be within easy reach of a bicycle ride if the roads are good and the itinerary flat. As such, the town may be considerably closer than a rocky mountaintop a couple of miles away. "An 'objectively' long path can be shorter than an 'objectively' much shorter path which is perhaps an 'onerous one' and strikes one as infinitely long".[6] In other words, measurements can be as exact as you like, without thereby being relevant and useful when it comes to determining genuine spatiality as manifested in our experiences and pragmatic dealings.

Heidegger's analysis reveals two very different notions of space. On the one hand, there is the exact, three-dimensional space of Euclidian geometry. On the other hand, there is space as it unfolds in Dasein's practical dealings with entities that are ready-to-hand. One might be tempted to suggest that geometric measurements give us an objective description of space as it really is, whereas a conception of space that relies on criteria such as ease and speed of access is subjectivist or, at best, anthropocentric. Heidegger, however, resists this suggestion and argues that the idea that physical space is more fundamental than pragmatic space simply reveals prior metaphysical commitments. The really real reality is precisely the one that is disclosed in and through Dasein's being-in-the-world. It is, according to Heidegger, precisely because space is accessible to us in a pragmatic context that it can be made the object of detached, scientific knowledge. In our concernful dealings with entities that are ready-to-hand, a need for more exact measurements may sometimes arise, for example, in the construction of buildings or bridges, or in the surveying of land. If one goes on to abstract completely from pragmatic interests, then space can become the object of mere observation and theorising.[7] Unsurprisingly, however, Heidegger claims that such an exclusive focus on the geometry of space involves a neutralisation of the originally given, pragmatically significant space. As Heidegger puts it, space thereby becomes "deprived of its worldliness".[8] The spatiality of the concrete context of concernful dealings is transformed into a pure dimensionality. Thereby, entities that are ready-to-hand lose their peculiar referential character, and the world is reduced to a conglomerate of extended things.

When discussing the spatiality of our pragmatic dealing with equipment, there is something that has constantly been presupposed without being explicitly thematised – namely, Dasein's *embodiment*. There is, however, one place in *Being and Time* where Heidegger explicitly mentions the body. This is in section 23, where he states that Dasein's own spatiality is connected to its "corporeality". He goes on to add, however, that the body "contains a problematic of its own not to be discussed here".[9] This silence regarding the body is puzzling, especially considering how Heidegger's own terminology – for example, the distinction between the ready-to-*hand* and the present-at-*hand* – draws constant attention to the fact that Dasein is embodied (e.g., has hands). Moreover, Heidegger's account of the concernful disclosure of space has, in a sense, been all about the body. The closeness or remoteness of some place or entity has precisely to do with its availability for use, the ease (or otherwise) with which it may be reached, and so on. All of this surely refers us to the working, grasping, walking – in short, embodied – subject.

It might be objected that it is both obvious and self-evident that Dasein is embodied, and that an explicit analysis, therefore, is superfluous. But surely such a reply is too facile. As Heidegger himself emphasises in the first section of *Being and Time*, in philosophy "the appeal to self-evidence [. . .] is a dubious procedure".[10] This is also the case when it comes to Dasein's embodiment, since an in-depth analysis hereof can in fact add decisively to our understanding of the mind–world relation, which is precisely what other phenomenologists, including Husserl, Sartre, and Merleau-Ponty, would argue.

THE LIVED BODY

Given a certain theoretical framework, it might seem obvious that the body is first and foremost a spatial object in the world. Just as we can perceive a bunch of grapes or a bonfire, we can see, touch, and smell the body. Is this also the view of phenomenologists? A phenomenological investigation of the body should presumably focus on the body as a phenomenon. But how exactly is the body given when we admire a painting or use the vacuum cleaner? How is it present? Is it among the perceptually available objects? Am I aware of my own body as a perceptual object in space? As Husserl, Merleau-Ponty, and Sartre all insist, the body is not simply one object among many. Its mode of appearance is in fact quite different from ordinary objects. Whereas I can approach and remove myself from spatial objects, the body is always present as that which makes it possible for me to adopt a perspective on the world. Indeed, the body is first and foremost this perspective on the world, and, therefore, not originally an object that I take a perspective on. To claim otherwise is to commence an infinite regress.[11] Sartre even writes that the lived body is invisibly present, precisely because it is existentially lived rather than known.[12]

Under normal circumstances, I do not need to perceive the hand visually in order to know where it is located. When I reach for the racket, I do not first have to search for the hand. I do not need to look for it, since it is always with me. I also don't need to look at myself to find out if I'm sitting up or lying down, or if my legs are crossed or not.

Let us consider a situation, where we are sitting in a restaurant. I wish to begin to eat, and so I need to pick up the fork and knife. But how can I do that? In order to pick up either, I need to know their position in relation to myself. That is, my perception of the fork and knife must contain some information about my own location, otherwise I would not be able to act on it. On the dinner table, the perceived fork is to the left (of me), the perceived knife is to the right (of me), and the perceived plate and wineglass in front (of me). The body is, consequently, characterised by being present in every perceptual experience as the experiential zero-point, the absolute "here" in relation to which every appearing object is oriented. The bodily "here" is not one point among many, but the anchor that makes other coordinates meaningful. Originally – i.e., pre-reflectively – the body is not given perspectivally, and I am not given to myself as existing in or as a spatial object. To claim otherwise is to misunderstand the true nature of our bodily existence:

> The problem of the body and its relations with consciousness is often obscured by the fact that while the body is from the start posited as a certain *thing* having its own laws and capable of being defined from outside, consciousness is then reached by the type of inner intuition which is peculiar to it. Actually if after grasping "my" consciousness in its absolute interiority and by a series of reflective acts, I then seek to unite it with a certain living object composed of a nervous system, a brain, glands, digestive, respiratory, and circulatory organs whose very matter is capable of being analyzed chemically into atoms of hydrogen, carbon, nitrogen, phosphorus, *etc.*, then I am going to encounter insurmountable difficulties. But these difficulties all stem from the fact that I try to unite my consciousness not with *my* body but with the body of *others*. For the body which I have just described is not *my* body such as it is *for me*.[13]

As an experiencing, embodied subject, I am the point of reference in relation to which all of my perceptual objects, be they near or far, left or right, up or down, are uniquely related:

> It is thus that all things of the surrounding world possess an orientation to the Body [. . .]. The "far" is far from me, from my Body; the "to the right" refers back to the right side of my Body, e.g., to my right hand. [. . .] I have all things over and against me; they are all "there" – with the exception of one and only one, namely the Body, which is always "here".[14]

I am the centre around which and in relation to which (egocentric) space unfolds itself, which is also why Husserl writes that every world-experience is enabled by our embodiment.[15] This is so, not only because the body functions as a stable centre of orientation, but also because of its mobility. We see with mobile eyes that are set in a head that can turn and which is attached to a body that can move from place to place; a stationary point of view is to that extent only the limiting case of a mobile point of view. What we see and hear and touch and taste and smell is shaped by what we do, and what we are capable of doing. A hammer is something I can grab and use. A log blocking the road is something I can climb over or sit on to rest. A frozen lake is something I can cross. We can instantly see if an object is within reach, if a doorway is big enough to walk through without having to bend down, if a chair is the right height to sit on, etc. This experience is body-related, it is not an experience of specific geometric measurements, but an assessment of whether the distance and size is appropriate vis-à-vis our own embodiment.

In ordinary experience, perception and movement are united. When I touch the surface of a sponge, the sponge is given in conjunction with an experience of the movement of the finger. When I observe the movement of the dancer on the scene, the dancer is given in conjunction with the experience of the movement of my head. This Husserlian line of argument can also be found in Merleau-Ponty and Sartre. Merleau-Ponty writes that when I perceive the world, the body is simultaneously revealed as the unperceived term in the centre of the world toward which all objects turn their face.[16] I do not observe the world from a distance, but I am placed right in its middle, and the world reveals itself according to our bodily ways of inhabiting it. Sartre speaks of how space is structured by *references of use* where the position and orientation of the individual objects are connected to an *acting* subject. That which is perceived is perceived as nearby or further away, as something that can be approached and explored. That the knife is lying there on the table means that I can reach and grasp it. The body is operative in every perception and in every action. It constitutes our *point of view* and our *point of departure*.[17]

> [T]he perceptive field refers to a center objectively defined by that reference and located *in the very field* which is oriented around it. Only we do not see this center as the structure of the perceptive field considered; *we are the center*. [. . .] Thus my being-in-the-world, by the sole fact that it *realizes* a world, causes itself to be indicated to itself as a being-in-the-midst-of-the-world by the world which it realizes. The case could not be otherwise, for my being has no other way of entering into contact with the world except *to be in the world*. It would be impossible for me to realize a world in which I was not and which would be for me a pure object of a surveying contemplation. [. . .] Thus to say that I have entered into the world, "come to the world", or that there is a world, or that I have a body is one and the same thing.[18]

When arguing that the body plays a decisive role in different forms of intentionality – when claiming that perception, for instance, is an essentially embodied activity – the important point is not that the subject can only perceive objects and employ tools if it *has* a body, but, rather, that it can only do so if it *is* a body, i.e., an embodied subjectivity. Or to put it differently, what has to be recognised is that the bodily "I can" constitutes a fundamental form of intentionality.

As Sartre points out, we should not let our investigation of the body be led by an external physiological perspective which ultimately has its origin in the anatomical study of the *corpse*.[19] A central distinction, already introduced by Husserl, is here the one between (a) our original unthematic, pre-reflectively lived body-awareness that accompanies and conditions every spatial experience, and

(b) the subsequent thematic experience *of* the body as an object. It is necessary to distinguish the body as it is subjectively lived through, and the body as an object among others. Whereas Husserl employs the concepts of *Leib* and *Körper*, Merleau-Ponty would later distinguish between *corps propre* and *corps objectif*. As Husserl insists, the latter form of body-awareness depends upon the former:

> Here it must also be noted that in all experience of things, the lived body is co-experienced as a functioning lived body (thus not as a mere thing), and that when it itself is experienced as a thing, it is experienced in a double way—i.e., precisely as an experienced thing and as a functioning lived body together in one.[20]

Obviously, the body can explore itself. It can take itself (or the body of another) as an object of exploration. This is what typically happens in physiology or neurology. But such an investigation of the body as an object is neither exhaustive, nor does it disclose the most fundamental nature of the body. The constitution of the body as an object is not an activity that is carried out by a disincarnate subject. It is a self-objectification effectuated by an embodied subject. The lived body precedes the perceived body. Originally, I do not have any consciousness *of* my body. I am not perceiving it, I *am* it.[21]

Whereas the body as object captures how the body is apprehended from an observer's point of view, where the observer might be a scientist, a physician, or even the embodied subject herself, the notion of a subjective body captures the way the body is lived through from an embodied first-person perspective. The distinction between the body as subject and the body as object is a phenomenological distinction. The idea is not that we each have two different bodies, but rather that we can experience and understand the same body in different ways.

But why is it that the tactually or visually explored body can still be experienced as the exteriority of *my own* body? This is where both Husserl and Merleau-Ponty highlight the importance of what they call double-sensation or double-touch. When my left hand touches my right hand, the left touching hand feels the surface of the right touched hand. But the touched right hand is not simply given as a mere object, since it feels the touch itself.[22] Moreover, the relation between the touching and the touched is reversible, since the right hand can also touch the left hand. It is this reversibility that demonstrates that the bodily interiority and exteriority are different manifestations of the same.[23] The phenomenon of double-touch consequently presents us with an ambiguous setting in which the hand alternates between two roles, that of touching and that of being touched. That is, the phenomenon of double-sensation provides us with an experience of the dual nature of the body. Sometimes, the locution *Leibkörper* is used to designate that kind of bodily self-experience.

Normally, our body tends to efface itself on its way to its intentional goal. We do not normally monitor our movements in an explicitly conscious manner. This is fortunate, for had we been aware of our bodily movements in the same way in which we are attentively aware of objects, our body would have made such high demands on our consciousness that it would have interfered with our daily life. When I write on my laptop, my movements are not given as intentional objects. My limbs do not compete for my attention. Had that been the case, I would not have been able to write efficiently. But, of course, things might change if something goes wrong. Consider a case discussed by Drew Leder. Imagine that you are playing tennis. Your attention is directed at the ball, which is heading towards you with high speed, as well as on the position of your opponent. Your body tightens in order to return the ball in a masterful smash, but suddenly you feel a sharp and intense pain in your arm. Your smashing opportunity is lost, and the pain is now demanding all your attention. It attracts your attention whether you want it to or not. Indeed, there might be nothing that reminds us as much of our embodiment (our vulnerability and mortality) as pain.[24] More generally speaking, the body is present in such a fundamental manner that we normally only notice it when our habitual and smooth interaction with the world is disturbed, be it by voluntary reflections (be they philosophical or specular), or by reflections that are forced upon us by sickness, bodily needs, exhaustion, or pain. As with so many other things in life, it is often deprivation that teaches us about the importance of that which we take for granted. It is when it no longer functions smoothly that we realise the fundamental role of the body.

Nothing in this conception of embodiment should lead us to think of the body as something static, as if it has a fixed set of skills and abilities. Not only can the body expand its sensorimotor repertoire by acquiring new skills and habits, it can even extend its capacities by incorporating artificial organs and parts of its environment. A classical case mentioned by Merleau-Ponty concerns the blind man and his cane.[25] When exploring the ground with the cane, the man does not feel the cane in his hand, but the ground in front of him. It is as if the borders of his sensing body have expanded and no longer stop at the skin.

The phenomenological investigation of the body is clearly not simply one analysis among many. It is not as if phenomenology, in its investigation of different kinds of objects, also stumbled upon the body and then proceeded to investigate it further. On the contrary, both Husserl and the French phenomenologists grant the body a special status, since it is taken to be deeply implicated in our relation to the world, in our relation to others, and in our self-relation.

Phenomenologists do not offer a solution to the classical mind–body problem: How does the body interact causally with the mind? Rather, they seek to understand to what extent our experience of the world, our experience of self, and our experience of others are formed by and influenced by our embodiment. But through this change of focus, they also rethink and question some of the distinctions that define the mind–body problem in the first place. The notion of embodiment, the notion of an embodied mind or a minded body, is meant to replace the ordinary notions of mind and body, both of which are considered derivations and abstractions. To put it differently, our bodily experience cannot neatly be categorised as either subjective or objective, inner or outer, physical or psychical. Whereas Husserl writes that the body is "simultaneously a spatial externality and a subjective internality",[26] Merleau-Ponty speaks of the ambiguous nature of the body and argues that bodily existence is a third category beyond the merely physiological and the merely psychological.[27]

To take embodiment seriously is to contest a Cartesian view of the mind in more than one way. Embodiment entails birth and death. To be born is not to be one's own foundation, but to be situated in both nature and culture. It is to possess a physiology that one did not choose. It is to find oneself in a historical and sociological context that one did not establish. Ultimately, the issues of birth and death enlarge the scope of the investigation. They call attention to the role of historicity, generativity, and sexuality.[28] Indeed, rather than being simply a biological given, embodiment is also a category of sociocultural analysis. To gain a more comprehensive understanding of the embodied mind, one cannot just focus narrowly on perception and action, one also has to consider sociality.

NOTES

1 Heidegger, M. (1996). *Being and Time*, trans. J. Stambaugh. Albany, NY: SUNY: 61.

2 Heidegger, M. (1996). *Being and Time*, trans. J. Stambaugh. Albany, NY: SUNY: 65.

3 Heidegger, M. (1996). *Being and Time*, trans. J. Stambaugh. Albany, NY: SUNY: 57.

4 Heidegger, M. (1996). *Being and Time*, trans. J. Stambaugh. Albany, NY: SUNY: 98.

5 Heidegger, M. (1996). *Being and Time*, trans. J. Stambaugh. Albany, NY: SUNY: 99.

6 Heidegger, M. (1996). *Being and Time*, trans. J. Stambaugh. Albany, NY: SUNY: 98–99.

7 One can find related considerations by Husserl in an appendix to *Crisis* entitled "The Origin of Geometry" (cf. Husserl, E. (1970). *The Crisis of European Sciences and Transcendental Phenomenology: An Introduction to Phenomenological Philosophy*, trans. D. Carr. Evanston, IL: Northwestern University Press: 353–378).

8 Heidegger, M. (1996). *Being and Time*, trans. J. Stambaugh. Albany, NY: SUNY: 104.

9 Heidegger, M. (1996). *Being and Time*, trans. J. Stambaugh. Albany, NY: SUNY: 101.

10 Heidegger, M. (1996). *Being and Time*, trans. J. Stambaugh. Albany, NY: SUNY: 3.

11 Sartre, J.-P. (2003). *Being and Nothingness*, trans. H.E. Barnes. London: Routledge: 353; Merleau-Ponty, M. (2012). *Phenomenology of Perception*, trans. D.A. Landes. London: Routledge: 93.

12 Sartre, J.-P. (2003). *Being and Nothingness*, trans. H.E. Barnes. London: Routledge: 348.

13 Sartre, J.-P. (2003). *Being and Nothingness*, trans. H.E. Barnes. London: Routledge: 327.

14 Husserl, E. (1989). *Ideas Pertaining to a Pure Phenomenology and to a Phenomenological Philosophy. Second Book. Studies in the Phenomenology of Constitution*, trans. R. Rojcewicz and A. Schuwer. Dordrecht: Kluwer Academic Publishers: 166.

15 Husserl, E. (1989). *Ideas Pertaining to a Pure Phenomenology and to a Phenomenological Philosophy. Second Book. Studies in the Phenomenology of Constitution*, trans. R. Rojcewicz and A. Schuwer. Dordrecht: Kluwer Academic Publishers: 61.

16 Merleau-Ponty, M. (2012). *Phenomenology of Perception*, trans. D.A. Landes. London: Routledge: 84.

17 Sartre, J.-P. (2003). *Being and Nothingness*, trans. H.E. Barnes. London: Routledge: 350.

18 Sartre, J.-P. (2003). *Being and Nothingness*, trans. H.E. Barnes. London: Routledge: 342.

19 Sartre, J.-P. (2003). *Being and Nothingness*, trans. H.E. Barnes. London: Routledge: 372.

20 Husserl, E. (1973a). *Zur Phänomenologie der Intersubjektivität II. Texte aus dem Nachlass. Zweiter Teil. 1921–1928*, ed. by I. Kern. Husserliana 14. The Hague: Martinus Nijhoff: 57.

21 Sartre, J.-P. (2003). *Being and Nothingness*, trans. H.E. Barnes. London: Routledge: 347.

22 Husserl, E. (1989). *Ideas Pertaining to a Pure Phenomenology and to a Phenomenological Philosophy. Second Book. Studies in the Phenomenology of Constitution*, trans. R. Rojcewicz and A. Schuwer. Dordrecht: Kluwer Academic Publishers: 152–153.

23 Husserl, E. (1973a). *Zur Phänomenologie der Intersubjektivität II. Texte aus dem Nachlass. Zweiter Teil. 1921–1928*, ed. by I. Kern. Husserliana 14. The Hague: Martinus Nijhoff: 75.

24 Leder, D. (1990). *The Absent Body*. Chicago, IL: University of Chicago Press.

25 Merleau-Ponty, M. (2012). *Phenomenology of Perception*, trans. D.A. Landes. London: Routledge: 144.

26 Husserl, E. (1977). *Phenomenological Psychology: Lectures, Summer Semester, 1925*, trans. J. Scanlon. The Hague: Martinus Nijhoff: 151.

27 Merleau-Ponty, M. (2012). *Phenomenology of Perception*, trans. D.A. Landes. London: Routledge: 204–205.

28 Heinämaa, S. (2003). *Toward a Phenomenology of Sexual Difference: Husserl, Merleau-Ponty, Beauvoir*. Lanham, MD: Rowman & Littlefield.

SUGGESTIONS FOR FURTHER READING

Luna Dolezal, *The Body and Shame: Phenomenology, Feminism, and the Socially Shaped Body*. Lanham, MD: Lexington Books, 2015.

Sara Heinämaa, *Toward a Phenomenology of Sexual Difference: Husserl, Merleau-Ponty, Beauvoir*. Lanham, MD: Rowman & Littlefield, 2003.

Drew Leder, *The Absent Body*. Chicago: Chicago University Press, 1990.

Joona Taipale, *Phenomenology and Embodiment: Husserl and the Constitution of Subjectivity*. Evanston, IL: Northwestern University Press, 2014.

8

INTERSUBJECTIVITY AND SOCIALITY

Has phenomenology anything of interest to say on the topic of intersubjectivity? As one frequently stated criticism has it, due to its preoccupation with subjectivity, phenomenology did not only fail to realise the true significance of intersubjectivity, but was also fundamentally incapable of addressing the issue in a satisfactory manner.[1] As a closer scrutiny of the writings of such figures as Scheler, Stein, Husserl, Heidegger, Gurwitsch, Sartre, Merleau-Ponty, and Levinas is bound to reveal, however, this criticism is quite misplaced. The truth of the matter is that intersubjectivity is ascribed an absolutely central role by phenomenologists. It is no coincidence that the first philosopher ever to subject the very notion of intersubjectivity (*Intersubjektivität*) to a systematic and extensive discussion was none other than Husserl.

Far from ignoring the issues of intersubjectivity and sociality, the phenomenological tradition contains rich but quite diverse and even occasionally competing accounts. Despite their diversity, it is still possible to point to certain distinctive features that can be found in most of the different approaches:

- Without ever denying the eminently intersubjective character of *language*, phenomenologists have often endeavoured to unearth

DOI: 10.4324/9781003350682-11

pre- or extra-linguistic forms of intersubjectivity, be it in perception, in tool use, in emotions, or body awareness.

- Phenomenologists never conceive of intersubjectivity as an objectively existing structure in the world that can be comprehensively described and analysed from a third-person perspective. On the contrary, intersubjectivity is a relation between subjects and its full analysis must include a reference to and an investigation of the first-person perspective.

- One of the crucial ideas found in many phenomenologists is that an account of intersubjectivity requires a simultaneous analysis of the relationship between subjectivity and world. That is, it is not satisfactory simply to insert intersubjectivity somewhere within an already established framework; rather, the three dimensions "self", "other", and "world" reciprocally illuminate one another and can only be fully understood in their interconnection. As Merleau-Ponty would put it, the subject must be seen as an embedded and embodied existence, and the world as a common field of experience, if intersubjectivity is at all to be possible.

It will be impossible to cover all facets of this rich discussion in the present chapter, but let me start with a point of common concern: The critical appraisal of the "argument from analogy".

THE PROBLEM OF OTHER MINDS

On some readings, the problem of intersubjectivity is really another name for the *problem of other minds*. Why should there be a problem? Because the only mind I allegedly have direct access to is my own. My access to the mind of another is, by contrast, always mediated by his or her bodily behaviour. But how could the perception of another person's body provide me with information about his mind? One of the classical attempts to come to grips with this problem is known as the *argument from analogy*. In my own case, I can observe that I have experiences when my body is causally influenced and that these experiences frequently bring about certain actions. I observe that other bodies are influenced and act in similar manners and I therefore infer through analogy that the behaviour of foreign bodies is probably associated with experiences similar to those I have myself. In my own case, being scalded by hot water is associated with the feeling of intense pain, this experience then gives rise to the quite distinct behaviour of screaming. When I observe other bodies being scalded by hot water and screaming, I assume that it is likely that they are also feeling pain. Thus, the argument from analogy can be interpreted as an inference to the best explanation, one that brings us from observed public behaviour to a hidden mental cause. Although this inference does not provide me with indubitable knowledge about others, and although it does not allow me to actually experience other minds, at least it gives me more reason to believe in their existence than in denying it.

This way of accounting for our understanding of others has not exactly been met with much enthusiasm by phenomenologists. They have all criticised it. The criticism has been multifaceted, but in Max Scheler's work *The Nature of Sympathy* and in Merleau-Ponty's essay "The Child's Relations with Others", we find some of the core objections.

As Scheler and Merleau-Ponty point out, by arguing that our understanding of others is inferential in nature, the argument from analogy opts for a cognitively far-too-demanding account. Infants (not to speak of non-human animals) are already from early on sensitive and responsive to facial expressions, posture, and intonation. But to suggest that the child compares the visual presentation of, say, the other's smile with the facial movements it itself makes when happy and that the infant then projects its own felt happiness into the invisible interiority of the other's body is psychologically implausible.[2]

Another concern that they also both raise is the following. In order for the argument from analogy to succeed, it has to rely on a similarity between the way in which my own body is given to me, and the way in which the body of the other is given to me. However, my own body as it is intero- and proprioceptively felt by me does not correspond point by point to the other's body as it is visually presented to me. Indeed, if I am to detect a similarity between, say, my laughing or screaming and the laughing or screaming of somebody else, I need to adopt a more global perspective. I need to understand the bodily gestures as expressive phenomena, as manifestations of joy or pain, and not simply as physical movements. But if such an understanding is required for the argument of analogy to succeed, the argument presupposes what it is supposed to establish. To put it differently, we only employ analogical lines of reasoning when we are already convinced that we are facing minded creatures, but simply remain unsure about precisely how we are to interpret the expressive phenomena in question.[3]

After these initial considerations, Scheler and Merleau-Ponty dig deeper in their criticism. Scheler, for his part, questions two crucial presuppositions in the argument from analogy. First, the argument assumes that my starting point is my own consciousness. This is what is given to me in a quite direct and unmediated fashion, and it is this purely mental self-experience that is then taken to precede and make possible the recognition of others. One is at home in oneself and one then projects onto the other, whom one does not know, what one already finds in oneself. Incidentally, this implies that one is only able to understand those psychological states in others that one has already experienced in oneself. Second, the argument assumes that we never have direct access to another person's mind. We can never *experience* her thoughts or feelings; we can only infer that they must exist based on what is actually presented to us, namely her bodily behaviour. Although these two assumptions may seem perfectly obvious, Scheler rejects both. As he points out, we should pay attention to what is actually given, rather than letting some theory dictate what can be given.[4] In Scheler's view, the argument from analogy overestimates the difficulties involved in the experience of others and underestimates the difficulties involved in self-experience.[5] We should not ignore what can be directly perceived about others, nor should we fail to acknowledge the embodied and embedded character of our own self-experience. Scheler consequently denies that our initial self-acquaintance is of a purely mental nature that precedes our experience of our own expressive movements and actions and that takes place in isolation from others. He also denies that our basic acquaintance with others is inferential in nature. As he argues, there is something highly problematic about claiming that intersubjective understanding is a two-stage process, of which the first stage is the perception of meaningless behaviour and the second an intellectually based attribution of psychological meaning. Such an account presents us with a distorted picture, not only of behaviour but also of the mind. It is no coincidence that we use psychological terms to describe behaviour and that we would be hard-pressed to describe the latter in terms of bare movements. In the majority of cases, it is quite difficult (and artificial) to divide a phenomenon neatly into a psychological and a behavioural aspect – think merely of a groan of pain, a handshake, an embrace. On the contrary, in the face-to-face encounter, we are not confronted with a mere body, or with a hidden psyche, but with a unified whole. Scheler occasionally speaks of an "expressive unity". It is only, subsequently, through a process of abstraction, that this unity can be divided, and our interest can then proceed "inwards" or "outwards".[6]

We find similar considerations in Merleau-Ponty, who not only argues that anger, shame, hate, and love, rather than being psychic facts which are hidden at the bottom of another's consciousness, are types of behaviour or styles of conduct that are visible from the outside. Such emotions exist, as Merleau-Ponty puts it, in the face or in those gestures, and not hidden behind them.[7] They are, in short, expressed in bodily gestures and actions and are thereby visible to others. Merleau-Ponty furthermore claims that the incapacity of classical psychology to provide a satisfactory solution to the problem of how we relate to others is due to the fact that it bases its entire approach on certain unquestioned and unwarranted philosophical prejudices. First and foremost among these is the fundamental assumption that experiential life is directly accessible to one person only, namely the individual who owns it, and that the only access one has to the psyche of another is indirect and mediated by his or her bodily appearance.[8] But Merleau-Ponty rejects the idea that my experiential life is a sequence of internal states that are inaccessible to anyone but me. Rather, in his view, our experiential life is, above all, a relation to the world, and it is in this comportment toward the world that I will also be able to discover the consciousness of the other. As he writes, the "perspective on the other is opened to me from the moment I define him and myself as 'conducts' at work in the world".[9] Merleau-Ponty consequently argues that we need to redefine our notion of psyche if we are to make it comprehensible how we can relate to and comprehend others.

Phenomenologists have, in general, taken an embodied perceptual approach to the questions of understanding others and the problem of intersubjectivity. We begin from the recognition that our perception of the other's bodily presence is unlike our perception of physical things. The other is given in his or her bodily presence as a lived body, a body that is actively engaged in the world. It is, indeed, as Sartre also points out, a decisive mistake to think that my ordinary encounter with the body of another is an encounter with the kind of body described by physiology. The body of another is always given to me in a situation or meaningful context, which is co-determined by the action and expressivity of that very body.[10]

EMPATHY

The criticism of the argument from analogy constitutes a focal point of agreement among various phenomenologists. Some of them, including Husserl and Stein, also suggest that our understanding of others draws on a distinct type of intentionality, which they call *empathy (Einfühlung)*.[11]

For phenomenologists, empathy is not to be conflated with emotional contagion, imaginative perspective-taking, sympathy, or compassion. Rather, they consider empathy a basic, perceptually-based form of other-understanding, one that other more complex and indirect forms of interpersonal understanding presuppose and rely on.

They consequently often used the term empathy interchangeably with terms such as other-experience or other-perception.[12] In their view, one can obtain an acquaintance with the other's experiential life in the empathic face-to-face encounter that has a directness and immediacy to it that is not shared by whatever beliefs you might have about the other in his or her absence. As Husserl writes, the mind of the other, his thinking, feeling, desiring, is intuitively present in the gestures, the intonation, and in the facial expressions. The expressivity of the other is imbued with psychological meaning from the start, and it is empathy that allows us to understand and grasp this psychological meaning.[13]

But is the experiential life of the other really given as directly to us as our own? As both Merleau-Ponty and Stein would insist, although I can perceive the grief or the anger of the other in his or her conduct, in his face or hands, the grief and the anger of the other will never quite have the same significance for me as they have for him. For me these situations are displayed, for him they are lived through.[14] Although empathy announces in the most direct manner possible, the actual presence of the other's experience, there will always, and by necessity, remain a difference between that which I am aware of when I empathise with the other, and that which the other is experiencing. To experience, say, the emotion of the other empathically consequently differs from the way you would experience the emotion if it were your own.[15]

This is also why Stein rejects the proposal that empathy literally involves the transmission of the other's experience into one's own mind. What is distinctive about empathy is precisely that the empathised experience is located in the other and not in oneself.[16] Empathy targets foreign experiences without eliminating their alterity. Rather than blurring the distinction between self and other, rather than leading to some kind of fusion or some sense of merged personal identities, the asymmetry between self-experience and other-experience is in this account crucial for empathy. Husserl occasionally talks of empathy as that which permits us to encounter true transcendence and writes that our consciousness in empathy transcends itself and is confronted with otherness of a completely new kind.[17]

When claiming that we are able to *experience* others, and as a consequence do not exclusively have to rely on and employ inferences, imitations, or projections, this is not meant to entail that we can experience the other in precisely the same way as she herself does, nor that the other's consciousness is accessible to us in precisely the same way as our own is. But when I experience the facial expressions or meaningful actions of another, I am still *experiencing* foreign subjectivity, and not merely imagining it, simulating it, or theorising about it. The fact that I can be mistaken and deceived is no argument against the experiential character of the access. Moreover, the fact that my experiential access to the minds of others differs from my experiential access to my own mind need not be an imperfection or shortcoming. On the contrary, it is precisely because of this difference, precisely because of this asymmetry, that we can claim that the minds we experience are *other* minds. As Husserl points out, had the consciousness of the other been given to me in the same way as my own, the other would cease being an other and would instead become a part of myself.[18] Indeed, a more precise way of capturing what is at stake might be by saying that when we experientially encounter other subjects, we always encounter others as subjects who surpass our grasp. Thus, the givenness of the other is of a most peculiar kind. The otherness of the other is precisely *manifest* in his or her elusiveness. As Levinas observed, the absence of the other is exactly his presence as other.[19] There is, so to speak, more to the mind of the other than what we are grasping, but this does not make our understanding non-experiential.

By allowing for the possibility of an experiential encounter with another's embodied and embedded experiences, phenomenologists stand opposed to dominant positions within the so-called theory of mind debate, i.e., the theory-theory of mind and the simulation theory of mind. Both of the latter positions deny that it is possible to experience the minds of others. It is precisely because of the absence of an experiential access to other minds that we need to rely on and employ either theoretical inferences or internal simulations. By contrast, phenomenologists would precisely insist that we can experience the other directly as a minded being, as a being whose bodily gestures and actions are expressive of his or her experiences or states of mind.[20]

BEING-WITH

Whereas many phenomenologists assigned crucial importance to empathy, not everybody did. One phenomenologist who was sceptical about its significance was Heidegger. For Heidegger, the notion of empathy was introduced in order to explain how one (isolated) subject could encounter and understand another (isolated) subject.[21] In his view, this approach fundamentally misconceived the nature of intersubjectivity, in that it took it to be first and foremost a thematic encounter between individuals, where one is trying to grasp the emotions or experiences of the other (this connotation is particularly obvious in the German word for empathy: *Einfühlung*). But as Heidegger points out, the very attempt to thematically grasp the experiences of others is the exception rather than the rule.

Ordinarily, we do not encounter others as thematic objects of cognition. Rather, we encounter them in the world in which our daily life occurs, or, to be more precise, we encounter others in a worldly situation, and our way of being together and understanding each other is co-determined in its meaning by the situation at hand. In fact, in our daily life of practical concerns we are constantly with others. We are living in a public world, and the work we do, the tools we use, the goals we pursue, all contain references to others, regardless of whether or not they are factually present: "The poorly cultivated field along which I am walking appresents its owner or tenant. The sailboat at anchor appresents someone in particular, the one who takes his trips in it".[22] Indeed, just as Dasein is not first a worldless subject to whom a world is then subsequently added, Dasein is not alone until another happens to turn up. The very suggestion that a bridge or connection has to be established between two initially independent selves, an I and a Thou, is altogether a fundamental misunderstanding. There is no gap to be bridged by empathy, since a basic constituent of Dasein's being-in-the-world is its *being-with*:

> It is assumed that a subject is encapsulated within itself and now has the task of empathizing with another subject. This way of formulating the question is absurd, since there never is such a subject in the sense it is assumed here. If the constitution of what is Dasein is instead regarded without presuppositions as in-being and being-with in the presuppositionless immediacy of everydayness, it then becomes clear that the problem of *empathy* is just as absurd as the question of the reality of the external world.[23]

Heidegger's criticism highlights three important issues: 1. It clearly shows that a phenomenological investigation of intersubjectivity cannot merely focus on the face-to-face encounter. 2. It raises the question of what is most fundamental, the concrete face-to-face encounter or life in a shared world. 3. It asks us to consider whether a satisfying account of intersubjectivity requires an emphasis on or rather an elimination of the difference between self and other.

As for the first issue, Heidegger was certainly not the only phenomenologist to make this claim. As Sartre explains, utensils incontestably refer to a plurality of *bodily* others by whom they have been manufactured and by whom they are used.[24] To that extent, the coexistence of others is already co-implied in our activities of taking care of matters and utilising things. As existing in-the-world, we constantly depend upon others:

> To live in a world haunted by my neighbor is not only to be able to encounter the Other at every turn of the road; it is also to find myself engaged in a world in which instrumental-complexes can have a meaning which my free project has not first given to them. It means also that in the midst of this world *already* provided with meaning I meet with a meaning which is *mine* and which I have not given to myself, which I discover that I "possess already".[25]

Hence, the existence of objects of use in the world indicates our membership in a community of subjects. In my use of equipment or instruments, my most immediate goals are those of anybody: I grasp myself as interchangeable with any of my neighbours, and do not distinguish myself from them. Ultimately, whenever I make use of an instrument that was manufactured by others for an anonymous consumer, i.e., for a sheer "someone", I forfeit my own individuality. Whenever I try on a pair of shoes, or uncork a bottle, or step into an elevator, or laugh in a theatre, I am, as Sartre writes, making myself into "anyone".[26] So far so good, but as Sartre then continues, we shouldn't forget that an object can only appear to me as a piece of equipment that "one" uses in such and such a manner, if I have been taught so by others that I have encountered concretely.[27] Related ideas can also be found in Husserl, who already in *Ideas II* pointed to the fact that, next to the tendencies originating from other persons, there also exist indeterminate general demands made by custom and tradition: "One" judges thus, "one" holds the fork in such and such a way, etc.[28] I learn what counts as normal from others – and, indeed, initially and for the most part from those closest to me, hence from those I grow up with, those who teach me, and those belonging to the most intimate sphere of my life. And it is in this way that I participate in a communal *tradition*. Husserl refers to *normal life* as *generative life*, and states that every (normal) human being is *historical* in virtue of being constituted as a member of a historically enduring community.[29] In the end, each new generation inherits what was constituted through the labour of previous generations, and by reshaping this heritage it then makes its own contribution to the constitution of the communal unity of the tradition. Community and communalisation inherently point beyond themselves to the open endlessness of the chain of generations, and this in turn points to the historicity of human existence itself.

As for the second issue, Schutz presents us with a balanced view. Schutz considers the direct face-to-face encounter basic in the sense that all other forms of interpersonal understanding derive their validity from this kind of encounter.[30] But as he keeps emphasising, interpersonal understanding comes in many forms and shapes, and if we wish to do justice to this variety and complexity we must go beyond what a narrow focus on empathy can deliver. Our understanding of others never takes place in a vacuum; it does not have the format of a snapshot. Ordinarily, we always bring a stock of knowledge to the encounter with the other, both knowledge of a more general sort, but frequently also knowledge regarding the particular person in question, knowledge of his habits, interests, etc.[31] This knowledge comes to serve as an interpretive scheme even in the case of direct social interaction. One can consequently accept the critical point made by Heidegger and still consider the notion of empathy to be useful. One should simply acknowledge that our typical understanding of others is contextual and realise that empathy, properly understood, is not a question of feelingly projecting oneself into the other, but rather an ability to experience behaviour as expressive of mind, i.e., an ability to access the life of the mind of others in their expressive behaviour and meaningful action.

As for the final issue, Sartre eventually voiced a harsh criticism of Heidegger's approach. To downplay or ignore the face-to-face encounter and to emphasise the extent to which our everyday being-with-one-another is characterised by anonymity and substitutability – as Heidegger puts it, the others are those among whom one is, but from whom "one mostly does not distinguish oneself"[32] – is, according to Sartre, to miss out on what is actually at stake in intersubjectivity: The encounter and confrontation with *radical otherness*. Sartre's highlighting of the alterity and transcendence of the other was subsequently radicalised by Levinas, who also attacked

Heidegger for offering a totalising account that failed to respect and appreciate the alterity and difference of the other.[33] In his own work, Levinas went on to argue that my encounter with the other is an encounter with something that cannot be conceptualised or categorised: "If one could possess, grasp, and know the other, it would not be other".[34] The encounter with the other is an encounter with an ineffable alterity. It is an encounter that is not conditioned by anything in my power, but which has the character of a visitation, an epiphany, or a revelation. In a characteristic move, Levinas then argued that the authentic encounter with the other, rather than being perceptual or epistemic, is *ethical* in nature.[35] For both Levinas and Sartre, an account of intersubjectivity will fail if it tries to eliminate the difference between self and other. For other phenomenologists, too much emphasis on the irreducible difference between self and other simply makes their relation and connection incomprehensible. As this impasse indicates, one of the decisive challenges facing a phenomenological account of intersubjectivity is to find the proper balance between the similarity and difference of self and other.

COMMUNITY

What we find in phenomenological work on sociality is not merely a discussion of how we come to understand each other. This initial work gradually gave rise to a rich discussion of larger group formations and eventually resulted in a targeted exploration of communal life. Interestingly, and perhaps not surprisingly given the different views just presented, it is also possible here to trace out two divergent phenomenological approaches. One insists that communal experiences and we-relationships are rooted in and dependent upon specific forms of interpersonal understanding, and that a proper phenomenological account of different group formations consequently requires an exploration of how individuals are experientially interrelated. The other argues that any privileging of the dyadic face-to-face relationship is bound to miss out on what is truly distinctive about communal life.

Let me, in turn, present and discuss these two competing views. As we have already seen, Scheler distinguishes our ability to directly grasp the minded life of others as it is perceptually manifest in their bodily expressivity from more indirect forms of analogical reasoning that we also occasionally employ. In his work, *The Nature of Sympathy*, Scheler goes on to offer a fine-grained taxonomy of different types of emotional relatedness, and highlights the distinctions between the following:

- Emotional contagion, where one is affected (or infected) by the emotional state of others, say, their joy or fear.
- Sympathy, which is an emotional response to the other's emotional state.
- Emotional sharing, which involves experiencing an emotion together with a co-subject as *ours*.[36]

In the work *Formalism in Ethics and Non-Formal Ethics of Values*, Scheler returned to these distinctions, but added that they are also operative in different social units, and that the task of a philosophical sociology is to develop a theory of how these different group formations are interrelated. To exemplify, Scheler distinguishes the *crowd*, which he takes to be ruled by emotional contagion, the *association*, which he considers an artificial unity of instrumentally interrelated distrustful individuals who employ analogical reasoning, and the *community*, which is characterised by emotional sharing, trust, and reciprocity.[37] A careful investigation and analysis of different forms of interpersonal relation and understanding is, consequently, considered an important stepping stone towards a phenomenology of social formations. Scheler's distinction between community and society can also be found in the work of Gerda Walther. Walther defines an association as an aggregation of individuals who decide to join forces out of purely strategic or instrumental considerations. A community, by contrast, is formed by individuals who understand themselves and the others as members of a *we*, and who are tied together by bonds of solidarity. More specifically, Walther talks about how a phenomenological investigation of the community must consider the nature and structure of we-experiences, and how the latter involve an inner bond, a feeling of togetherness, or a reciprocal unification between its members. As Walther writes: "Only with their inner bond, with that feeling of togetherness – even if loose and limited – is a social formation transformed into a community".[38]

But how is this inner bond or unification brought about? It is revealing here that Walther explicitly acknowledges the extent to which her own investigation presupposes and builds upon the analyses of empathy offered by previous phenomenologists.[39] More specifically, she discusses how we-experiences come to be felt not as mine or yours, but as *ours*, as a result of a process of interlocking acts of reciprocal empathy.[40]

The idea that a special kind of reciprocal empathy might play a crucial role in the development of a we-perspective is also to be found in Husserl.

In manuscripts from the early twenties and thirties, Husserl argues that my empathic experience of another, who is, in turn, experientially directed at myself, such that my experience of the other involves a co-experience of myself, is a condition of possibility for we-acts.[41] Husserl explores what happens when I address the other and when the other is aware that he is being addressed and when he reciprocates. When both of us become aware that we are being experienced and understood by the other, we are dealing with communicative acts through which a higher interpersonal unity – a we – can be established.[42] Husserl consequently emphasises the centrality of dialogue for the constitution of the we, and speaks of communication as a community-creating act.[43]

Not everybody, however, would agree with this insistence on the importance of embodied dyadic relations for communal experiences. In the work of Heidegger and Gurwitsch, we find various criticisms. Given what has earlier been said about Heidegger's position, his criticisms should not come as a surprise. Not only does Heidegger deny that empathy has any ontological or epistemic primacy, he explicitly argues that: "The with-one-another cannot be explained through the I-Thou relation".[44]

Heidegger acknowledges that there are many ways in which people can come together, from a nameless and revolting mass, to a bowling team, or a band of robbers. But as long as we think simply of the we as a plurality, as an "assembly of individual human beings",[45] or as a "multitude of separate Is",[46] we will, in his view, not have grasped what a genuine community is.[47] In a lecture from

1934, Heidegger goes on to argue that the we, the people, the *Volk*, doesn't come about because several independent subjects agree to establish a community. Rather, it is always already decided, based on shared history and descent.[48]

A somewhat comparable criticism can also be found in the work of Gurwitsch. Gurwitsch takes issue with Walther's reference to a feeling of togetherness and argues that one should recognise not only that strategic associations can sometimes occur accompanied by positive feelings, but also that a community is not necessarily threatened or undermined in cases where conflicts or feuds take the place of positive sentiments. Membership of a community can consequently persist even when negative interpersonal emotions are present. But if a feeling of togetherness is not what constitutes a community qua community, what is then decisive? For Gurwitsch, the essential factor is the presence of a shared tradition. Whereas strategic partnerships can be voluntarily initiated and discontinued, one is born into and brought up within a community, and this communal membership is not something from which one can voluntarily dissociate oneself.[49] In fact, it is quite beyond the domain of personal will and decision. Those with whom one is communally joined have not been selected by free choice based on their personal qualities, but rather based on a shared heritage. Communalisation is, consequently, essentially historical. Our membership in a community deeply influences the way we understand both the world and ourselves by rooting us in a context that is taken for granted.[50]

The phenomenological debate about the foundations of sociality did not end with the contributions of Heidegger and Gurwitsch. The discussion of whether dyadic face-to-face encounters or more anonymous and communal forms of being-with-one-another have priority continues to this day.[51]

NOTES

1 Habermas, J. (1992). *Postmetaphysical Thinking*, trans. W.M. Hohengarten. Cambridge, MA: MIT Press.
2 Scheler, M. (2008). *The Nature of Sympathy*, trans. P. Heath. London: Transaction: 239.
3 Gurwitsch, A. (1979). *Human Encounters in the Social World*. Pittsburgh, PA: Duquesne University Press: 14, 18.

4 Scheler, M. (2008). *The Nature of Sympathy*, trans. P. Heath. London: Transaction: 244.

5 Scheler, M. (2008). *The Nature of Sympathy*, trans. P. Heath. London: Transaction: 250–252.

6 Scheler, M. (2008). *The Nature of Sympathy*, trans. P. Heath. London: Transaction: 261.

7 Merleau-Ponty, M. (1964b). *Sense and Non-Sense*, trans. H. Dreyfus and P. Dreyfus. Evanston, IL: Northwestern University Press: 52–53.

8 Merleau-Ponty, M. (1964c). *The Primacy of Perception*, ed. by J.M. Edie. Evanston, IL: Northwestern University Press: 113, 114.

9 Merleau-Ponty, M. (1964c). *The Primacy of Perception*, ed. by J.M. Edie. Evanston, IL: Northwestern University Press: 117.

10 Sartre, J.-P. (2003). *Being and Nothingness*, trans. H.E. Barnes. London: Routledge: 369.

11 See, for instance, Stein, E. (1989). *On the Problem of Empathy*, trans. W. Stein. Washington, DG: ICS Publications.

12 Husserl, E. (1960). *Cartesian Meditations: An Introduction to Phenomenology*, trans. D. Cairns. The Hague: Martinus Nijhoff: 92; Scheler, M. (2008). *The Nature of Sympathy*, trans. P. Heath. London: Transaction: 220.

13 Husserl, E. (1989). *Ideas Pertaining to a Pure Phenomenology and to a Phenomenological Philosophy. Second Book. Studies in the Phenomenology of Constitution*, trans. R. Rojcewicz and A. Schuwer. Dordrecht: Kluwer Academic Publishers: 247, 256

14 Merleau-Ponty, M. (2012). *Phenomenology of Perception*, trans. D.A. Landes. London: Routledge: 372.

15 Stein, E. (1989). *On the Problem of Empathy*, trans. W. Stein. Washington, DC: ICS Publications: 10.

16 Stein, E. (1989). *On the Problem of Empathy*, trans. W. Stein. Washington, DC: ICS Publications: 10.

17 Husserl, E. (1973a). *Zur Phänomenologie der Intersubjektivität II. Texte aus dem Nachlass. Zweiter Teil. 1921–1928*, ed. by I. Kern. Husserliana 14. The Hague: Martinus Nijhoff: 8–9, 442.

18 Husserl, E. (1960). *Cartesian Meditations: An Introduction to Phenomenology*, trans. D. Cairns. The Hague: Martinus Nijhoff: 109.

19 Levinas, E. (1987). *Time and the Other*, trans. R.A. Cohen. Pittsburgh, PA: Duquesne University Press: 94.

20 For more on the difference between phenomenological approaches to social cognition and mainstream positions in the theory-of-mind debate, see Gallagher, S. (2007). Simulation trouble. *Social Neuroscience* 2(3–4): 353–365 and Zahavi, D. (2011). Empathy and direct social perception. A phenomenological proposal. *Review of Philosophy and Psychology* 2(3): 541–558.

21 Heidegger, M. (2001). *Einleitung in die Philosophie*. Gesamtausgabe Band 27. Frankfurt am Main: Vittorio Klostermann: 145.

22 Heidegger, M. (1985). *History of the Concept of Time: Prolegomena*, trans. T. Kisiel. Bloomington, IN: Indiana University Press: 240.

23 Heidegger, M. (1985). *History of the Concept of Time: Prolegomena*, trans. T. Kisiel. Bloomington, IN: Indiana University Press: 243.

24 Sartre, J.-P. (2003). *Being and Nothingness*, trans. H.E. Barnes. London: Routledge: 363, 365.

25 Sartre, J.-P. (2003). *Being and Nothingness*, trans. H.E. Barnes. London: Routledge: 531.

26 Sartre, J.-P. (2003). *Being and Nothingness*, trans. H.E. Barnes. London: Routledge: 448.

27 Sartre, J.-P. (2003). *Being and Nothingness*, trans. H.E. Barnes. London: Routledge: 449.

28 Husserl, E. (1989). *Ideas Pertaining to a Pure Phenomenology and to a Phenomenological Philosophy. Second Book. Studies in the Phenomenology of Constitution*, trans. R. Rojcewicz and A. Schuwer. Dordrecht: Kluwer Academic Publishers: 281–282.

29 Husserl, E. (1973b). *Zur Phänomenologie der Intersubjektivität III. Texte aus dem Nachlass. Dritter Teil. 1929–1935*, ed. by I. Kern. Husserliana 15. The Hague: Martinus Nijhoff: 138–139, 431.

30 Schutz, A. (1967). *The Phenomenology of the Social World*, trans. G. Walsh and F. Lehnert. Evanston, IL: Northwestern University Press: 162.

31 Schutz, A. (1967). *The Phenomenology of the Social World*, trans. G. Walsh and F. Lehnert. Evanston, IL: Northwestern University Press: 169.

32 Heidegger, M. (1996). *Being and Time*, trans. J. Stambaugh. Albany, NY: SUNY: 111.

33 Levinas, E. (1969). *Totality and Infinity: An Essay on Exteriority*, trans. A. Lingis. Pittsburgh, PA: Duquesne University Press: 45–46, 67–68, 89.

34 Levinas, E. (1987). *Time and the Other*, trans. R.A. Cohen. Pittsburgh, PA: Duquesne University Press: 90.

35 Levinas, E. (1969). *Totality and Infinity: An Essay on Exteriority*, trans. A. Lingis. Pittsburgh, PA: Duquesne University Press: 43.

36 Scheler, M. (2008). *The Nature of Sympathy*, trans. P. Heath. London: Transaction: 8, 12–13, 15.

37 Scheler, M. (1973). *Formalism in Ethics and Non-Formal Ethics of Values: A New Attempt Toward a Foundation of an Ethical Personalism*, trans. M.S. Frings and R.L. Funk. Evanston, IL: Northwestern University Press: 525–529.

38 Walther, G. (1923). Zur Ontologie der sozialen Gemeinschaften. In E. Husserl (ed.), *Jahrbuch für Philosophie und Phänomenologische Forschung*, Vol. *VI* (pp. 1–158). Halle: Max Niemeyer: 33.

39 Walther, G. (1923). Zur Ontologie der sozialen Gemeinschaften. In E. Husserl (ed.), *Jahrbuch für Philosophie und Phänomenologische Forschung*, Vol. *VI* (pp. 1–158). Halle: Max Niemeyer: 17.

40 Walther, G. (1923). Zur Ontologie der sozialen Gemeinschaften. In E. Husserl (ed.), *Jahrbuch für Philosophie und Phänomenologische Forschung*, Vol. *VI* (pp. 1–158). Halle: Max Niemeyer: 85.

41 Husserl, E. (1959). *Erste Philosophie (1923/24). Zweiter Teil. Theorie der Phänomenologischen Reduktion*, ed. by R. Boehm. Husserliana 8. The Hague: Martinus Nijhoff: 136–137.

42 Husserl, E. (1989). *Ideas Pertaining to a Pure Phenomenology and to a Phenomenological Philosophy. Second Book. Studies in the Phenomenology of Constitution*, trans. R. Rojcewicz and A. Schuwer. Dordrecht: Kluwer Academic Publishers: 202–204, 254.

43 Husserl, E. (1973b). *Zur Phänomenologie der Intersubjektivität III. Texte aus dem Nachlass. Dritter Teil. 1929–1935*, ed. by I. Kern. Husserliana 15. The Hague: Martinus Nijhoff: 473. See also Meindl, P. and Zahavi, D. (2023). From communication to communalization: A Husserlian account. *Continental Philosophy Review* 56(3): 361–377.

44 Heidegger, M. (2001). *Einleitung in die Philosophie*. Gesamtausgabe Band 27. Frankfurt am Main: Vittorio Klostermann: 145–146.

45 Heidegger, M. (2009). *Logic as the Question Concerning the Essence of Language*, trans. W.T. Gregory and Y. Unna. Albany, NY: SUNY: 55.

46 Heidegger, M. (2009). *Logic as the Question Concerning the Essence of Language*, trans. W.T. Gregory and Y. Unna. Albany, NY: SUNY: 34.

47 Heidegger, M. (2009). *Logic as the Question Concerning the Essence of Language*, trans. W.T. Gregory and Y. Unna. Albany, NY: SUNY: 45.

48 Heidegger, M. (2009). *Logic as the Question Concerning the Essence of Language*, trans. W.T. Gregory and Y. Unna. Albany, NY: SUNY: 50, 72.

49 Gurwitsch, A. (1979). *Human Encounters in the Social World*. Pittsburgh, PA: Duquesne University Press: 122–124.

50 Gurwitsch, A. (1979). *Human Encounters in the Social World*. Pittsburgh, PA: Duquesne University Press: 132.

51 Schmid, H.B. (2009). *Plural Action. Essays in Philosophy and Social Science*. Dordrecht: Springer; Zahavi, D. (2019). Second-person engagement, self-alienation, and group-identification. *Topoi* 38: 251–260.

SUGGESTIONS FOR FURTHER READING

Anna Bortolan and Elisa Magrì (eds.), *Empathy, Intersubjectivity, and the Social World*. Berlin: De Gruyter, 2022.

Michael Theunissen, *The Other: Studies in the Social Ontology of Husserl, Heidegger, Sartre and Buber*, trans. C. Macann. Cambridge, MA: MIT Press, 1986.

Dan Zahavi, *Being We: Phenomenological Contributions to Social Ontology*. Oxford: Oxford University Press, 2025.

9

CRITICAL AND POLITICAL PHENOMENOLOGY

Recent years have seen the emergence of what has become known as *critical phenomenology*. Although this development has undeniably led to a renewed interest in phenomenology, it continues to remain contentious what precisely critical phenomenology is and how it differs from classical phenomenology.

One decisive motivation for the "critical turn" has been a desire for social and political transformation. Phenomenology shouldn't merely be descriptive but rather aim for a more just and inclusive social order. Phenomenology can offer a philosophically distinctive approach to social critique and should be used to illuminate, analyse, and ultimately oppose social injustice, marginalisation, racism, colonialism, ableism, homophobia, etc. Critical phenomenology is a form of critical theory that seeks to challenge conditions and mindsets that result in oppression, exclusion, and domination, but is critical phenomenology also critical of classical phenomenology?

Let me in the following outline some of the main controversies surrounding the term and then exemplify how the critical perspective has enriched phenomenological analyses of embodiment.

Although one can find earlier occurrences of the term, recent references to *critical phenomenology* can be traced back to a 2013 text

DOI: 10.4324/9781003350682-12

by Lisa Guenther, where she argued that critical phenomenology continues "the phenomenological tradition of taking first-person experience as the starting point for philosophical reflection" while at the same time resisting the tendency of classical phenomenologists "to privilege transcendental subjectivity over transcendental intersubjectivity".[1] In her own work, Guenther has drawn explicitly on Merleau-Ponty and Levinas, and in later texts it has become evident that the one figure she primarily has in mind when talking of classical phenomenology is Husserl, who she claims has defended views that are "rather unhelpful [. . .] for the project of critical phenomenology".[2] Her main objections concern Husserl's privileging of individual subjectivity, his one-sided account of the process of constitution, where "consciousness constitutes the world without reciprocity",[3] his failure to recognise how profoundly contingent historical and social structures can shape the meaning and manner of our experience, and his reluctance to engage in any kind of normative critique.[4]

Guenther's critical remarks, which partially mirror how Heideggerians and Merleau-Pontians have in the past sought to locate a clear break between Husserlian and post-Husserlian phenomenology, have in turn given rise to a heated debate about the merits of her criticism and about the pertinence of the very distinction between classical phenomenology and critical phenomenology. Let us start with the former.

Even if Husserl did assign a certain independence to individual subjectivity – he would never claim that it is socially constructed or determined through and through – Husserl was not defending the view that the "first-person singular is absolutely prior to intersubjectivity".[5] On the contrary, a central and repeated claim of Husserl is that there are dimensions of individual subjectivity that only emerge in and through social interaction and which therefore depend upon intersubjectivity. As Husserl, for instance, writes, I only come to be a "personal subject, come to attain personal 'self-consciousness', in the I-you relation".[6] At the same time, and this is one of the most distinct features of his transcendental phenomenology, Husserl considered intersubjectivity crucial for the constitution of worldly objectivity.[7] Far from offering an account of constitution that ascribes absolute power to a free-standing sub-ject, Husserl also repeatedly emphasised the role of facticity and passivity and viewed subjectivity as a necessary rather than suffi-cient constitutive principle.[8] Indeed, Husserl's very conception of genetic phenomenology, his view that intentional structures have a temporal becoming, and that the accumulation and sedimenta-tion of past experiences shape and form the structure of our inten-tional life, is one exemplification of the reciprocal feedback that Guenther claims is missing in his phenomenology. A characteristic feature of Husserl's later thinking is that he came to appreciate the constitutive significance of factors such as generativity, tradition, historicity, and cultural normality. For one example among many, consider written language. As Husserl argued in a famous appendix to *Crisis*, the highest level of objectivity, scientific objectivity, can only be constituted the moment written meaning can be handed down from one generation to the next and thereby become incor-porated into the body of knowledge, which generations of scien-tists draw on and add to. By serving as a reservoir of knowledge, writing consequently has a major constitutive impact, and complex scientific theories that in many ways influence our daily life would never have been possible were it not for the historically contingent invention of writing.[9] As for the final issue about Husserl's lack of normative critique, his alleged lack of interest in engaging with and transforming the norms of the lifeworld,[10] Husserl did not only write extensively on social ethics, but was also deeply concerned with the possibility of a cultural renewal that, as Jansen puts it, "would be able to 'repair' the increasingly '*menschenverachtende*'", i.e., inhumane, "attitude that he witnessed coming to dominate European and specifically German society".[11]

At this point, however, one might reasonably ask "so what?" Why should it matter if Guenther's assessment of Husserl is flawed? Well, if even as classical a phenomenologist as Husserl held the views in question, what is then the merit of drawing a sharp distinction between classical and critical phenomenology? Moreover, to use the term critical phenomenology as a contrast term might suggest that classical phenomenology was somehow uncritical. But wasn't a central idea common to Husserl, Heidegger, and Merleau-Ponty precisely the idea that phenomenological philosophising must involve a critical reflection on unquestioned styles of thought, be it naturalism, objectivism, or other traditional metaphysical mindsets? Merleau-Ponty even characterised phenomenology as a perpetual critical (self-)reflection, that shouldn't take anything for granted, least of all itself. A natural reply to this point would then be to say that we need to distinguish different styles of criticism, and that even if classical phenomenology might have been critical towards specific styles of thinking, it wasn't sufficiently politically engaged, it wasn't sufficiently critical of specific socio-political practices. The problem with this specific reply is that it gets history wrong. As the recent *Routledge Handbook of Political Phenomenology* documents, the events of the First World War and its aftermaths led to what has been described as a politicisation of early phenomenology. Not only do we find figures like Husserl, Scheler, and Heidegger engaging with topics such as nationalism, liberalism, and capitalism, we also find extensive phenomenological analyses of community, state, and law. One of Husserl's assistants, Arnold Metzger, even wrote a treatise entitled *Phenomenology of Revolution*.

Admittedly, it is possible to find a diversity of positions represented. Many of the early phenomenologists were critical of capitalist-consumerist modernity and longed for a social rebirth and transformation, but whereas Husserl in one interpretation was drawn to a form of utopian anarchism,[12] others opted for socialism, Catholic conservatism, or even National Socialism, as was infamously the case for Heidegger, Oskar Becker, and Else Voigtländer. But the fact remains that the philosophical work of the early German phenomenologists does contain an engagement with social and political topics.[13]

If anything, this orientation only became even more pronounced in post-war French phenomenology, but there it also takes the form of an explicit social critique. The Second World War, the German occupation, and the ensuing emergence of the Cold War, intensified the political commitments of Sartre, Merleau-Ponty, and Beauvoir. In 1946 Sartre published an essay entitled *Anti-Semite and Jew*.[14] The text was a discussion of anti-Semitism and one of the first philosophical treatments of the Holocaust. In 1949, Simone de Beauvoir published her major work *The Second Sex*,[15] which contained a phenomenological account of the gendered body, and in 1952 the psychiatrist Frantz Fanon published his renowned *Black Skin, White Masks* which criticised French colonialism and racism and offered a phenomenological analysis of the racialised body.[16]

Husserl's phenomenological analyses were initially very generic. For Husserl, it was a matter of investigating what characterises consciousness as such. In later phases of his thinking, Husserl became increasingly interested in the question of how cultural, historical, and developmental conditions affect our intentional life. It is this movement from the ahistorical to the historically situated that is continued in both Sartre and Merleau-Ponty and subsequently radicalised by thinkers such as Beauvoir and Fanon.

Given considerations like these, one must wonder about the merits of a sharp distinction between classical and critical phenomenology. Perhaps Salamon was precisely right when she at one point wrote that "what is critical about critical phenomenology turns out to have been there all along".[17] Rather than distinguishing two types of phenomenology, it probably makes more sense to say that phenomenology is constantly evolving and that the work of both classical phenomenologists as well as more recent phenomenological authors can be used for different purposes including the purpose of social critique. This also seems to be the view that is gaining traction. In recent publications, Lanei Rodemeyer and Johanna Oksala both argue that Husserl along with Beauvoir and Fanon should be considered central thinkers for critical phenomenology.[18] And in a recent excellent introduction to critical phenomenology, Elisa Magrí and Paddy McQueen are very explicit about the extent to which critical methodological approaches can already be found in classical phenomenology.[19]

MARGINALISED EXPERIENCES

In their introduction to *50 Concepts for a Critical Phenomenology*, Weiss, Murphy, and Salamon write that a critical phenomenology is a phenomenology that seeks to "encourage generosity, respect, and compassion for the diversity of our lived experiences".[20] This focus on the need for offering a more comprehensive account of diverse life experiences has indeed been one of the hallmarks of recent work in critical phenomenology.

When looking at some of the classical discussions of, say, our embodied being-in-the-world, they often occurred at a fairly high level of abstraction, with no reference to the age, sex, gender, or social position of the subject. But not only does this miss out on crucial aspects of lived experience, what was presented as a general account of embodiment often turned out to be nothing but, or so the argument goes, a universalisation of a very particular perspective, namely that of a male, white, and able-bodied subject.

A comprehensive phenomenological account of embodiment should recognise the extent to which bodily intentionality is influenced by gender, race, sexuality, and class and thematise how various societal and cultural practices influence one's bodily stance. When Husserl, Merleau-Ponty, and Sartre discussed the difference between the body as subject and the body as object, when they highlighted the importance of the bodily "I can", and when they argued that the body as lived through from a first-person perspective normally remains in the background, as non-objectified, this analysis might indeed capture something important, but it arguably also fails to account for some very salient bodily experiences.

In her book *The Imperative of Integration*, Elizabeth Anderson recounts a personal episode of hers. She was driving late at night in Detroit, when her oil light came on. She pulled into the nearest gas station to investigate further, and was then approached by a young black man, who wanted to offer to help her with her car. But rather than simply saying so, he said "Don't worry, I'm not here to rob you", while holding up his hands, palms flat at face level.[21] As Anderson explains, this interaction was clearly framed and influenced by racial stereotypes and stigmatisation, but as one might add, so was the bodily intentionality of the young man. Rather than being able to offer his help carefree and spontaneously, he had to be aware of how he appeared to others and in particular had to appraise how his movements might be interpreted by a white woman.

The classical phenomenological analysis of racial oppression, of how the internalisation of a white gaze and white norms transforms one's being-in-the-world and restricts, inhibits, and objectifies one's bodily existence, can, as already mentioned, be found in Fanon's *Black Skin, White Masks*. As Sara Ahmed was later to summarise succinctly:

> If classical phenomenology is about "motility", expressed in the hopefulness of the utterance "I can", Fanon's phenomenology of the black body would be better described in terms of the bodily and social experience of restriction, uncertainty and blockage, or perhaps even in terms of the despair of the utterance "I cannot". [. . .] To be black in "the white world" is to turn back towards itself, to become an object, which means not only not being extended by the contours of the world, but being diminished as an effect of the bodily extensions of others.[22]

But racism is not the only reason why a comprehensive phenomenological analysis of our bodily existence should also consider the historical, cultural, and social context. In a classical essay from 1980 "Throwing like a girl", which in turn engages with earlier texts by Erwin Straus, Merleau-Ponty, and Beauvoir, Iris Marion Young argued that women in patriarchal societies are often defined and regarded as mere bodies, as potential objects for other subjects' intentions and manipulations. The internalisation of this generalised attitude can come to affect women's own bodily existence, which will increasingly come to include components of self-objectification.[23] In addition, whereas (some) men might move and act with ease, historical forms of socialisation and enculturation have also installed specific norms and practices for how women are supposed to move and act that have diminished their agency and undermined their trust in their own capacities. As a result, women have come to approach many situations with timidity and hesitancy which is why their bodily intentionality in such contexts is more characterised by an "I cannot" or "I shouldn't" than by an "I can".[24] As Young is at pains to point out, the distinct modalities of feminine bodily comportment that she describes are not due to particularities of female anatomy or physiology, let alone rooted in some mysterious feminine essence, but are culturally informed styles of behaviour.[25]

Recent work by critical phenomenologists has extended the scope and analysed many other forms of oppressed and marginalised modes of existence. But it is worth emphasising that this laudable work, which has gone on to influence discussions in, for instance, critical disability studies, trans and queer studies, and postcolonial studies, is better seen as a continuation and expansion of work already starting in the late forties and early fifties rather than as constituting a marked departure from classical phenomenology.

THE PROBLEM OF METHOD

One of the questions currently being discussed is the extent to which a critical use of phenomenology necessitates a fundamental rethinking of its basic tools, concepts, and methods. Guenther, for one, has insisted that critical phenomenology must rethink the purpose and practice of the eidetic and transcendental methods and in the end go beyond what classical phenomenology has to offer if it wants to engage critically with history and power.[26]

The insistence on factoring in the specificities of the sociocultural context, for instance, raises various methodological questions. How do the analyses of, say, the racialised or gendered body stand to the more generic discussions of embodiment that we find in Husserl, Sartre, and Merleau-Ponty? Do the former analyses replace or rather supplement the latter? Is it at all possible to offer any kind of eidetic analysis of embodiment, any analysis that captures something that holds true for embodied existence in general or are there in the end only particular bodies such that what a phenomenological analysis can at most hope to accomplish is to offer an account of "a woman's body, a Latina's body, a mother's body, a daughter's body, a friend's body, an attractive body, an aging body, a Jewish body"?[27] Ultimately, it is hard to see how embodiment could still be susceptible to philosophical analysis if any reference to universal and invariant structures was prohibited. It is also hard to see why formal distinctions like the ones between the lived body and the objectified body or between reflective and pre-reflective body-awareness should no longer be able to target basic structures of human embodiment even if they might be further specified by more context-oriented investigations, or why general reflections on, say, the relation between perception, movement, and action or the role of bodily expressivity for interpersonal understanding, shouldn't continue to be of value.

It is after all one thing to argue that an analysis of embodiment that doesn't factor in the role of age, gender, race, etc. is incomplete, and something completely different to argue that such an analysis is at best worthless and at worst dangerously misleading. Young clearly took her own analysis to concretise and supplement, rather than replace, what could be found in Merleau-Ponty:

> I assume that at the most basic descriptive level, Merleau-Ponty's account of the relation of the lived body to its world, as developed in the *Phenomenology of Perception*, applies to any human existence in a general way. At a more specific level, however, there is a particular style of bodily comportment which is typical of feminine existence, and this style consists of particular modalities of the structures and conditions of the body's existence in the world.[28]

The focus on and interest in contingent historical and social structures has also raised questions about the transcendental status of phenomenology and led some to question the relevance of the phenomenological reduction. Johanna Oksala, by contrast, has been adamant that a phenomenology that wants to offer a fundamental form of social critique must employ the phenomenological reduction and lay bare how the world we live in rather than simply being a natural given is in fact the outcome of a process of constitution. After all, one of the aims of philosophical critique is to question social practices and beliefs that have become so sedimented that they are often accepted as unquestioned truths, as ontological facts, rather than being recognised for what they are, namely deeply rooted prejudices.[29]

For Guenther, critical phenomenology is not a science, but an open-ended practice, a way of approaching political activism,[30] and given this aspiration, it must also draw on methods coming from "postcolonial theory, feminism, critical race theory, Marxism, the Frankfurt school, psychoanalysis, queer theory, Foucaultian genealogy, deconstruction, critical disability studies, or some other critical discourse".[31] There might be good reasons for favouring methodological and theoretical pluralism, but if critical phenomenologists end up distancing themselves from both the transcendental reduction and the eidetic reduction, and if they instead seek inspiration from a variety of other disciplinary perspectives, it will at some point become urgent to specify exactly what it is that is supposed to make critical phenomenology phenomenological. Is a simple appeal to and interest in lived experience supposed to be sufficient? As we shall see in the next chapters, related discussions have also been taking place within the field of applied phenomenology.

NOTES

1 Guenther, L. (2013). *Solitary Confinement*. Minneapolis, MN: University of Minnesota Press: xv.

2 Guenther, L. (2020). Critical phenomenology. In G. Weiss, A.V. Murphy, and G. Salamon (eds.), *50 Concepts for a Critical Phenomenology* (pp. 11–16). Evanston, IL: Northwestern University Press: 12–13.

3 Guenther, L. (2020). Critical phenomenology. In G. Weiss, A.V. Murphy, and G. Salamon (eds.), *50 Concepts for a Critical Phenomenology* (pp. 11–16). Evanston, IL: Northwestern University Press: 12.

4 Guenther, L. (2020). Critical phenomenology. In G. Weiss, A.V. Murphy, and G. Salamon (eds.), *50 Concepts for a Critical Phenomenology* (pp. 11–16). Evanston, IL: Northwestern University Press: 12; Guenther, L. (2021). Six senses of critique for critical phenomenology. *Puncta: Journal of Critical Phenomenology* 4(2): 7.

5 Guenther, L. (2013). *Solitary Confinement*. Minneapolis, MN: University of Minnesota Press: xiii.

6 Husserl, E. (1973a). *Zur Phänomenologie der Intersubjektivität II. Texte aus dem Nachlass. Zweiter Teil. 1921–1928*, ed. by I. Kern. Husserliana 14. The Hague: Martinus Nijhoff: 171.

7 Zahavi, D. (2001). *Husserl and Transcendental Intersubjectivity*, trans. E. Behnke. Athens, OH: Ohio University Press.

8 Zahavi, D. (2017). *Husserl's Legacy: Phenomenology, Metaphysics, and Transcendental Philosophy*. Oxford: Oxford University Press: 108–136.

9 Husserl, E. (1973b). *Zur Phänomenologie der Intersubjektivität III. Texte aus dem Nachlass. Dritter Teil. 1929–1935*, ed. by I. Kern. Husserliana 15. The Hague: Martinus Nijhoff: 224; Husserl, E. (1970). *The Crisis of European Sciences and Transcendental Phenomenology: An Introduction to Phenomenological Philosophy*, trans. D. Carr. Evanston, IL: Northwestern University Press: 358–362.

10 Guenther, L. (2021). Six senses of critique for critical phenomenology. *Puncta: Journal of Critical Phenomenology* 4(2): 7.

11 Jansen, J. (2022). Phenomenology and critique: On "mere" description and its normative dimensions. In A.S. Aldea, D. Carr, and S. Heinämaa (eds.), *Phenomenology as Critique: Why Method Matters* (pp. 44–55). London: Routledge: 51.

12 Hart, J. (1992). *The Person and the Common Life: Studies in a Husserlian Social Ethics*. Dordrecht: Kluwer Academic Publishers.

13 Loidolt, S. (2024). Plural beginnings, ambivalent heritage. In S. Herrmann, G. Thonhauser, S. Loidolt, T. Matzner, and N. Baratella (eds.), *The Routledge Handbook of Political Phenomenology* (pp. 11–17), London: Routledge.

14 Sartre, J.-P. (1995). *Anti-Semite and Jew*, trans. G.J. Becker. New York, NY: Shocken Books.

15 Beauvoir, S. de (1953). *The Second Sex*, trans. H.M. Parshley. London: Jonathan Cape.

16 Fanon, F. (2008). *Black Skin, White Masks*, trans. C.L. Markmann. London: Pluto Press.

17 Salamon, G. (2018). What is critical about critical phenomenology? *Puncta: Journal of Critical Phenomenology* 1: 13.

18 Rodemeyer, L.M. (2022). A phenomenological critique of critical phenomenology. In A.S. Aldea, D. Carr, and S. Heinämaa (eds.), *Phenomenology as Critique: Why Method Matters* (pp. 95–112). London: Routledge: 110; Oksala, J. (2023). The method of critical phenomenology: Simone de Beauvoir as a phenomenologist. *European Journal of Philosophy* 31(1): 146.

19 Magrì, E. and McQueen, P. (2023). *Critical Phenomenology: An Introduction*. Cambridge: Polity Press.

20 Weiss, G., Murphy A. V., and Salamon, G. (2020). *50 Concepts for a Critical Phenomenology*. Evanston, IL: Northwestern University Press: xiv.

21 Anderson, E. (2010). *The Imperative of Integration*. Princeton, NJ: Princeton University Press: 53.

22 Ahmed, S. (2007). A phenomenology of whiteness. *Feminist Theory* 8(2): 161.

23 Young, I.M. (1980). Throwing like a girl: A phenomenology of feminine body comportment, motility and spatiality. *Human Studies* 3: 154.

24 Young, I.M. (1980). Throwing like a girl: A phenomenology of feminine body comportment, motility and spatiality. *Human Studies* 3: 146.

25 Young, I.M. (1980). Throwing like a girl: A phenomenology of feminine body comportment, motility and spatiality. *Human Studies* 3: 152.

26 Guenther, L. (2021). Six senses of critique for critical phenomenology. *Puncta: Journal of Critical Phenomenology* 4(2): 8.

27 Weiss, G. (1999) *Body Images: Embodiment as Intercorporeality*. London and New York, NY: Routledge: 1.

28 Young, I.M. (1980). Throwing like a girl: A phenomenology of feminine body comportment, motility and spatiality. *Human Studies* 3: 141.

29 Oksala, J. (2023). The method of critical phenomenology: Simone de Beauvoir as a phenomenologist. *European Journal of Philosophy* 31(1): 141–142.

30 Guenther, L. (2020). Critical phenomenology. In G. Weiss, A.V. Murphy, and G. Salamon (eds.), *50 Concepts for a Critical Phenomenology* (pp. 11–16). Evanston, IL: Northwestern University Press: 15.

31 Guenther, L. (2021). Six senses of critique for critical phenomenology. *Puncta: Journal of Critical Phenomenology* 4(2): 8.

SUGGESTIONS FOR FURTHER READING

Steffen Herrmann, Gerhard Thonhauser, Sophie Loidolt, Tobias Matzner, and Nils Baratella (eds.), *The Routledge Handbook of Political Phenomenology*. London: Routledge, 2024.

Elisa Magrì and Paddy McQueen, *Critical Phenomenology: An Introduction*. Cambridge: Polity Press, 2023.

Johanna Oksala, "The method of critical phenomenology: Simone de Beauvoir as a phenomenologist." *European Journal of Philosophy* 31(1), 2023, 137–150.

Gail Weiss, Ann V. Murphy, and Gayle Salamon (eds.), *50 Concepts for a Critical Phenomenology*. Evanston, IL: Northwestern University Press, 2020.

PART III

APPLIED PHENOMENOLOGY

At its core, phenomenology is a philosophical endeavour. Its task is not to expand the scope of our empirical knowledge, but rather to step back and investigate the fundamental structures, relations and capacities that are presupposed by any such empirical investigation. As Heidegger once remarked, "to philosophize means to be entirely and constantly troubled by and immediately sensitive to the complete enigma of things that common sense considers self-evident and unquestionable".[1] Indeed, according to one reading it is precisely this domain of ignored obviousness that phenomenology seeks to investigate, and its ability to do so is premised on its adoption of a specific philosophical attitude.

Given the distinctly philosophical nature of this venture, one might wonder whether phenomenology can offer anything of value to empirical science. Can it at all inform empirical work? As I will show in the following chapters, the answer to these questions is very much in the affirmative.

NOTE

1 Heidegger, M. (2010). *Logic: The Question of Truth*, trans. T. Sheehan. Bloomington, IN: Indiana University Press: 18.

10

CLASSICAL APPLICATIONS
Psychology, psychiatry, sociology

Phenomenology has been a source of inspiration for the empirical sciences and the world beyond academic philosophy from the very start. By offering an account of human existence, where the subject is understood as an embodied and socially and culturally embedded being-in-the-world, phenomenology has not only been able to analyse and illuminate a framework that is operative in scientific practice, it has also been able to offer crucial inputs to a variety of disciplines. Psychology and psychiatry were among the first to take inspiration from Husserl's call to attend to the phenomena,[1] but since then, many other disciplines and practices, including sociology, anthropology, comparative literature, architecture, nursing, and even quantum mechanics, have engaged with and drawn on ideas from phenomenology. More recently, phenomenology has also proven an important source of inspiration for theoretical debates in qualitative research, for embodied cognitive sciences, and for disciplines such as disability studies and critical race theory.

The applicability of phenomenology has been part of its enduring appeal, but how does applied phenomenology differ from non-applied or pure phenomenology, and what is the best way to practice and use phenomenology in a non-philosophical context? The very notion of applied phenomenology is admittedly somewhat ambiguous

DOI: 10.4324/9781003350682-14

and can be understood to mean different things. In the following, I will understand the notion of applied phenomenology to refer to cases where a non-philosophical discipline or practice adopts or incorporates ideas from philosophical phenomenology. In some cases, this impact has been so extensive and enduring that the discipline in question has received the designation "phenomenological". On this reading, exemplary cases of applied phenomenology would include, for instance, *phenomenological psychology, phenomenological psychiatry*, and *phenomenological sociology*.

However, one of the recurrent challenges has been to determine how deeply rooted in phenomenological philosophy a discipline or practice should be in order to qualify as phenomenological. How many of the core commitments of phenomenology would it have to accept? And is the influence primarily of a methodological nature, or rather to be found in the theoretical framework being employed? When looking back at discussions from the last 100 years, one will look in vain for a clear consensus.

In this chapter, I will provide a few examples of rather different classical applications of phenomenology. In the next chapters, I will then touch upon some of the more principled questions that the notion of applied phenomenology has given rise to, and briefly discuss some current controversies.

PHENOMENOLOGICAL PSYCHOLOGY

That phenomenology has close links to psychology should not come as a surprise. What are the historical origins? One obvious starting point would be Vienna in the 1880s. After all, that is where Husserl attended lectures by Franz Brentano (1838–1917), the prominent psychologist and philosopher, who had written on intentionality and insisted that a scientific psychology had to include careful descriptions of consciousness. In some of Husserl's earliest works, we even find Husserl characterising his own work as a form of descriptive psychology – a characterisation he was soon to regret, however, since it failed to recognise the distinct philosophical character of his own endeavour.[2] Later on, Husserl went on to distinguish two different phenomenological approaches to consciousness. On the one hand, we have *transcendental phenomenology*, and on the other, we have what he calls *phenomenological psychology*.³ How does the latter differ from the former? Both deal with consciousness, but they do so with rather different agendas in mind. For Husserl, the task of phenomenological psychology is to investigate intentional consciousness in a non-reductive manner, i.e., in a manner that respects its peculiarity and distinctive features. Phenomenological psychology is a psychology that takes the first-person perspective seriously, but which – in contrast to transcendental phenomenology – remains within the natural attitude. The phenomenological psychologist is, for Husserl, not a philosopher, but a scientist that leaves certain fundamental questions unasked.

What is the relevance of this distinction? Although Husserl was primarily interested in the development of philosophical phenomenology, he was not blind to the fact that his analyses might have ramifications for and be of pertinence to the psychological study of consciousness. Indeed, as he points out in his *Amsterdam Lectures* from 1928, if psychology is to develop in a scientifically rigorous manner, it needs a proper understanding and conception of experiential life, and this is precisely what phenomenology can offer. Phenomenology returns us to the experiential phenomena themselves, rather than making do with mere speculations and theories about their nature. In addition, phenomenology can supply psychology with a fundamental clarification of its basic concepts (attention, intention, perception, content, etc.). As Husserl writes, the phenomenological psychologist should suspend theoretical prejudices originating from other scientific disciplines in order to focus on what is given and with the aim of obtaining insights into the correlation between act and object.⁴

Although Husserl wrote about phenomenological psychology, it was for him never an end in itself, but rather always a means to something else, namely philosophical phenomenology. As he writes in *Crisis*, "there must be a way whereby a concretely executed psychology could lead to a transcendental philosophy".⁵ On occasions, Husserl even emphasises the propaedeutic advantages of approaching philosophical phenomenology through phenomenological psychology. As he puts it, one might start out with no interest whatsoever in transcendental philosophy, and merely be concerned with establishing a strictly scientific psychology. If this task is pursued in a radical manner, and if the structures of consciousness are investigated with sufficient precision and care, it will eventually be necessary to take the full step, to make a transcendental turn, and thereby reach philosophical phenomenology.[6]

When assessing Husserl's work on phenomenological psychology, it is consequently important to bear in mind that Husserl's primary interest was in the question of how to facilitate the entry into proper philosophical thinking, and not in providing concrete instructions of how to do experiments or conduct interviews. Already early on, however, Husserl's work became a source of inspiration for empirically oriented psychologists. One noteworthy figure is David Katz (1884–1953) who explicitly acknowledged his debt to Husserl. Katz attended Husserl's lectures and seminars in Göttingen and is primarily known for his major contributions to the phenomenology of touch and colour.

A distinctive and unifying feature of Katz's work was his enduring interest in human experience and the world of the phenomena. As MacLeod wrote in his obituary, for Katz any psychologist "should begin by deliberately 'bracketing' his physical, physiological, and philosophical biases and attempt to observe phenomena as they are actually presented".[7] Katz himself described his own method as that of an "unprejudiced description of the phenomena"[8], and as he put it in his introduction to *The World of Colour*:

> It is impossible to describe the totality of colour-phenomena without at the same time neglecting all other points of view from which colours might be studied. If one is to accomplish such a task one has to adhere rigorously and exclusively to the descriptive phenomenological point of view [. . .]. The modes of appearance of colour in space and the phenomena of illumination stand central in the studies reported in this book. The fact that illumination could in any sense at all be considered an independent psychological problem was not recognized until a phenomenologically trained eye was directed toward illumination as an independent *phenomenon*.[9]

Importantly, Katz was not opposed to or disinterested in quantitative research and mainstream psychological theory. Indeed, for Katz, phenomenological psychology was not about simply taking things at face value and avoiding the rigors of experimentation and theory construction. On the contrary, it was something that required careful training and discipline, and which could then lead to better experiments and better theorising. Through his attempt to provide undistorted descriptions of the phenomena as they appeared, Katz managed to disclose subtle nuances of ordinary human experience, that until then had been overlooked by other experimental psychologists. In his work on touch, for instance, he meticulously distinguished surface touch, immersed touch, and volume touch,[10] thereby pointing to the difference between sensing a two-dimensional surface structure, immersing your hand in different types of liquids and experiencing a tactual phenomenon with no definite shape or pattern, and feeling an underlying bone fracture by palpating the skin surface. Katz also made important contributions to the study of the link between movement and touch and argued that movement is as indispensable to touch as light is to vision.[11]

Katz was only one of the first in an illustrious line of phenomenologically influenced psychologists who offered important and illuminating analyses of various domains of human experience. Initially, most were active in Germany, but many were forced to emigrate in the thirties, and after the war the influence spread and there were active environments in, for instance, Switzerland, France, the Netherlands, Denmark, Sweden, and the US.[12] Important figures included Erwin Straus (1891–1975), Johannes Linschoten (1925–1964), and Franz From (1914–1998), who in turn contributed to our comprehension of spatiality, sleep, and interpersonal understanding.[13]

PHENOMENOLOGICAL PSYCHIATRY

Phenomenology also soon came to influence the field of psychiatry. Consider, for example, the early contributions of Karl Jaspers (1883–1969), who, before his career as an influential existential philosopher, worked as a psychiatrist. Already in 1912, Jaspers published a short article where he outlined how psychiatry could profit from Husserlian ideas.[14] In the following decades prominent psychiatrists such as Ludwig Binswanger (1881–1966), Eugène Minkowski (1885–1972), and Medard Boss (1903–1990) all engaged with phenomenology in their research and practice.

Given its subject matter, this development was to some extent quite natural. If we consider some of the central experiential categories that are afflicted in different psychopathological conditions, such as the character of temporal and spatial experience, the structure of intentionality, the experience of one's own body, the unity and identity of self, and the character of social engagement, the relevance of the phenomenological resources should be obvious. As we have already seen, phenomenology offers extensive analyses of these topics, and such analyses contain valuable material for any psychiatrist who is interested in understanding the experience of the patient. That such an understanding is needed, and that psychiatry can only make progress if it takes the experiential claims and concerns of the patients seriously, was precisely a conviction shared by the early phenomenological psychiatrists. Such a person-centred approach can be contrasted with another approach in psychiatry, one that largely sidelined the interest in and concern for the experiential life of the patients and instead turned to neurology and neurobiology in an attempt to determine the "real" underlying causes of the mental disorders. At its most extreme, such a brain-centred approach would consider symptoms reported by the patients as unreliable indicators of the underlying causes and argue that one should investigate the brain rather than speak with the patient, if one really wished to study and understand the disorders in question.

Let me here focus on the contribution of Eugène Minkowski, whom R.D. Laing would later describe as "the first figure in psychiatry to bring the nature of phenomenological investigation clearly into view".[15] After obtaining his medical degree in 1909, Minkowski studied philosophy and attended lectures by Pfänder and Geiger, two of Husserl's former students. He eventually became chief psychiatrist at the Sainte-Anne hospital, a leading psychiatric hospital in Paris.

In Minkowski's work, *Lived Time: Phenomenological and Psychopathological Studies*, published in 1933, we find explicit reflections on the question of whether and how one ought to make use of philosophical phenomenology in clinical practice and research. As Minkowski observed, there are those for whom the term "philosophical" has pejorative connotations. In his own case, however, insights from phenomenology had been of crucial value for his clinical practice and allowed him to expand his psychiatric knowledge. By employing a phenomenological framework and approach, it had been possible to gain some access to the otherwise unfathomable world of the patient.[16]

One of Minkowski's central claims was that the psychiatrist in order to offer a proper diagnosis should not merely observe and describe the frequency and regularity of the symptoms. Such symptoms, say, florid delusions or hallucinations, would in his view only present us with the surface of the disorder. They vary from individual to individual and are ultimately secondary and compensatory reactions to what must be considered the more fundamental core of the disorder. The task of the psychiatrist is to go beyond these scattered surface symptoms and relate them to the existential alterations of the patient's very being-in-the-world.[17]

As an illustration, Minkowski points to the difference between patients with schizophrenia and patients with paralytic dementia when it comes to their grasp of the "me-here-now". Whereas the latter might no longer know anything about their own autobiography, profession, civil status, etc., and typically lack knowledge of where they are and what date and time it is objectively speaking, they have no problem indicating that they are here right now by pointing to themselves or by tapping their feet at the ground. Patients with schizophrenia by contrast, might have detailed knowledge about the objective facts, about their history, profession, and the exact place and time, but do not feel subjectively connected to the here and now. As Minkowski puts it, the words "I exist" no longer have any precise sense for them. Minkowski consequently talks of how the fundamental framework of "me-here-now" is morbidly affected in schizophrenia.

More specifically, Minkowski took schizophrenia to involve what he called a fundamental *loss of vital contact with reality*.[18] To lose this ability is to lose the ability to "resonate with the world". It is to lose the ability to grasp the significance of objects, situations, events, and other people automatically and effortlessly. Because of this loss, individuals with schizophrenia might be puzzled by matters that seem obvious to most people and as a result find themselves in pervasive states of perplexity. Everything becomes a matter of rumination and deliberation.

One of the reasons Minkowski became interested in phenomenology was precisely because he thought it capable of uncovering and analysing such altered structures. At the same time, however,

Minkowski also emphasised how philosophical phenomenology might learn from its engagement with psychiatry. By constantly being oriented toward the concreteness of the patient's experiential life, psychiatry could help steer philosophy away from empty abstractions and speculations. Psychiatric research might even lead to a refinement of the phenomenological analyses, insofar as it called attention to specific aspects or dimensions that had hitherto been ignored. By disclosing various experiential anomalies, the psychiatrist could not only help the philosopher distinguish accidental regularities from truly essential features but also bring the taken-for-granted, unnoticed conditions of normal existence, be it at the level of intentionality, intersubjectivity, or self-experience, into sharp relief through a study of their pathological distortions.

Minkowski's discussion of the relation between phenomenology and psychiatry is an early illustration of what would later be called a relationship of mutual illumination or mutual enlightenment.[19] In a best-case scenario, to apply phenomenology is not simply a question of importing readymade ideas from one side to the other; is not simply a one-way street from philosophy to psychiatry or psychology, but a two-way exchange, where both sides might profit from the interaction and grow as a result.

At the same time, however, Minkowski was certainly not overlooking the difference between philosophy and psychiatry and was explicitly warning against any overly naive take on their compatibility. As he wrote at one point:

It was never a question of transposing purely and simply the data and methods used by a given philosopher into the realm of psychopathological facts. That would have led inevitably to a "hyperphilosophizing" of psychopathology, a danger I carefully avoided and against which I warned my young colleagues who were following in my path; it would have risked deforming psychopathology entirely.[20]

PHENOMENOLOGICAL SOCIOLOGY

As was pointed out in Chapter 8, phenomenologists have devoted a lot of time to the analysis of the topics of intersubjectivity and sociality, and at one point Husserl even argued that a proper development of phenomenology would lead to a kind of philosophical sociology.[21] Generally speaking, one can easily see phenomenology as a form of meta- or proto-sociology. By offering a fundamental account of human social existence, phenomenology is offering an elucidation of the framework within which the social sciences operate. Or, to put it differently, and even more concisely, a convincing theory of social reality requires an account of human (inter)subjectivity, which is something phenomenology can offer. As it turns out, however, one can also find a distinct tradition within sociology that draws from classical phenomenology when it comes to its themes and concepts.

Let us first look at a key figure, namely Alfred Schutz (1899–1959), who is often considered the founder of phenomenological sociology. Schutz originally studied law and obtained his doctorate in Vienna in 1921. Subsequently, he found work in a bank, and it was not until 1943, after his emigration to the USA, that Schutz obtained a part-time position at a university, namely at the *New School for Social Research* in New York. In 1952 he became a professor at the same institution.

Schutz was initially inspired by Max Weber's sociology, but although Weber regarded meaningful action as the central topic of the social sciences, Weber did not pursue more fundamental questions regarding the constitution of social meaning, and it was this lacuna that Schutz attempted to fill by enriching and expanding Weber's theory with ideas drawn from Husserl's phenomenology.

Since it is the lifeworld rather than the world of science that constitutes the frame and stage of social relations and actions, the sociologist, Schutz argued, should take her point of departure from the former. What was needed is precisely a systematic study of everyday life, and for Schutz this called for a new type of sociological theory. More specifically, Schutz's concrete contribution, which can already be found in his most well-known work *The Phenomenology of the Social World* from 1932, was on the one hand to describe and analyse the essential structures of the lifeworld and on the other to offer an account of the way in which subjectivity is involved in the construction of social meaning. Drawing on Husserl's analyses of intentionality, Schutz claimed that the social world reveals and manifests itself in various intentional experiences. Its meaningfulness is constituted by subjects, and in order to understand and scientifically address the social world, it is therefore necessary to examine the social agents for whom it exists. Absent individual subjects, in a mindless universe, there would be no social reality. For Schutz, the primary object of sociology is consequently not institutions, market conjunctures, social classes, or structures of power, but *human beings*, i.e., acting and experiencing individuals, considered in their myriad relations to each other, but also with an eye to their own, meaning-constituting subjective lives. Schutz's point, of course, is not that sociology should have no interest whatsoever in institutions, power structures, classes, and the like. But he warned against reifying and absolutising such societal structures. Human subjectivity is not merely moulded and determined by social forces. In interaction with others, subjectivity also shapes social reality. The task of a phenomenological sociology is to understand the workings of this constitutive process, and to clarify how social agents make sense of the world in which they live.[22]

How, then, does Schutz describe and characterise our daily life in the social world? One central notion of his is that of *typification*. When adults navigate the lifeworld, they operate with a repertoire of maxims, rules, and recipes for how to handle various situations and for how the world should be understood. This is not a matter of theoretical rationality, but rather of a form of practical "know-how" that specifies what "one" does in a given situation and provides us with the sense that we can rely on social reality and that others also experience it in a similar manner. The primary source of this knowledge is previous experiences – both experiences we have had ourselves, and experiences transmitted to us by others. As Schutz remarks at one point, none of us choose our place of birth, our mother tongue, the social and economic status of our parental family, or the conception of the world that is taken for granted by the group within which we are socialised. We all find ourselves situated within a preconstituted system of typifications, roles, and positions that are not of our own making, but part of our social heritage.[23]

Typifications do not merely affect how we understand the world but also play a key role in how we understand others. To see why, it is first important to realise that the social world is heterogeneous and that the same holds true for interpersonal understanding. The latter differs, depending on whether the ones we seek to understand are bodily present, or, rather, removed in space and time. It depends on whether the others belong to the world of our associates, contemporaries, predecessors, or successors, or to use Schutz's original terms, whether the others belong to our *Umwelt*, *Mitwelt*, *Vorwelt*, or *Folgewelt*.[24] The social world is multilayered, and one of the important tasks of a phenomenological sociology is to conduct a careful analysis of these different strata.

Let us take a closer look at the way we engage with our contemporaries – that is, those with whom we co-exist in time, but who we do not experience directly since they are not present in our immediate surroundings. Whereas face-to-face relationships involve a direct experience of the other, even if it can be very casual – say, a chance meeting with a stranger on the train – our understanding of our contemporaries is by definition indirect and will always draw on our general knowledge of the social world and be shaped and framed by structures of typicality.[25] As Schutz writes:

> Putting a letter in the mailbox, I expect that unknown people, called postmen, will act in a typical way, not quite intelligible to me, with the result that my letter will reach the addressee within typically reasonable time. Without ever having met a Frenchman or a German, I understand "Why France fears the rearmament of Germany." Complying with a rule of English grammar, I follow a socially approved behavior pattern of contemporary English-speaking fellow-men to which I have to adjust my own behavior in order to make myself understandable. And, finally, any artifact or utensil refers to the anonymous fellow-man who produced it to be used by other anonymous fellow-men for attaining typical goals by typical means.[26]

As the quote makes clear, many social processes do not merely involve typifications of others. They often also force me to typify my own actions. When posting a letter, I try to write in such a way that a typical postal worker will be able to decipher my handwriting, I write the address in a typical place on the envelope, etc. Briefly put, I try to make myself the typical "sender of a letter".[27] In this way, social typification and (self-)categorisation facilitates everyday predictability and makes it easier to navigate the social world.

Our everyday sense-making is also marked by the fact that knowledge is socially distributed. All of us know something about certain things, but very little about other things. A person can be an expert in Finno-Ugric languages and have no idea what to do if he cannot start his car. Fortunately, others (mechanics) do know how to deal with this sort of thing. And most of us have sufficient knowledge, even outside our fields of expertise, to get by in everyday life. We know how to fill up the tank and we have some rough knowledge of how to find someone who can fill the gaps in our own stock of knowledge.[28]

Schutz often stressed that the social distribution of knowledge was a topic that had been insufficiently studied and that it might also be labelled a "sociology of knowledge".[29] Originally, sociology of knowledge was a discipline that primarily addressed epistemological issues, such as how true knowledge is acquired, by which methods, etc. Its focus was on theoretical ideas and the knowledge of the "elite". Schutz, however, emphasised that also the mechanic and the supermarket check-out assistant have their own kind of knowledge and that such knowledge is just as legitimate an object for a genuine sociology of knowledge as is the knowledge of the scientific and cultural elite.[30]

In *The Social Construction of Reality: A Treatise in the Sociology of Knowledge*, two former students of Schutz, Peter L. Berger and Thomas Luckmann, argued that it is the task of a sociology of knowledge to analyse the societal conditions for the formation and maintenance of various types of knowledge, scientific as well as quotidian. They shared Schutz's basic intuitions. The sociology of knowledge is, briefly put, interested in how knowledge is produced, distributed, and internalised; it examines how the validity of any form of knowledge – be it that of the Tibetan monk, the American businesswoman, or the Dutch criminologist – is socially established.[31] But as Berger and Luckmann also stressed:

> [T]he sociology of knowledge must first of all concern itself with what people "know" as "reality" in their everyday, non- or pre-theoretical lives. In other words, common-sense "knowledge" rather than "ideas" must be the central focus for the sociology of knowledge. It is precisely this "knowledge" that constitutes the fabric of meanings without which no society could exist.[32]

Berger and Luckmann rejected any attempt to view social reality as a self-standing natural entity, as a non-human or supra-human *thing*.[33] As they write, the social order is a product of human activity; it is neither biologically determined, nor in any other way determined by facts of nature: "Social order is not part of the 'nature of things', and it cannot be derived from the 'laws of nature'. Social order exists *only* as a product of human activity".[34] The task of social theory is to provide an account of how human beings, through manifold forms of interaction, create and shape social structures and institutions, which may first have the character of a common, intersubjective reality, but eventually become "externalised" and achieve objective status. As Schutz would also say, this happens largely through institutionalised typifications.[35] Through institutionalisation, human activity is subjected to social control. The constructed social structures define what is normal, and sanctions are introduced to maintain the social order and avoid deviation. With time, institutions come to appear inevitable and objective. Yet:

> It is important to keep in mind that the objectivity of the institutional world, however massive it may appear to the individual, is a humanly produced, constructed objectivity [. . .]. The institutional world is objectivated human activity, and so is every single institution. [. . .] The paradox that man is capable of producing a world that he then experiences as something other than a human product will concern us later on. At the moment, it is important to emphasize that the relationship between man, the producer, and the social world, his product, is and remains a dialectical one. That is, man (not, of course, in isolation but in his collectivities) and his social world interact with each other. The product acts back upon the producer.[36]

Thus, social reality is not only an externalised and objectified human product, it also acts back upon human beings. Not only in the sense that we may feel it as an oppressive external force that we cannot resist, but also in the sense that social reality is something individual human beings "internalise". We are not raised outside society, but grow up within it. And as we grow up and mature, we adopt roles, attitudes, and norms from others.[37] Human society, Berger and Luckmann emphasise, must therefore be "understood in terms of an ongoing dialectic of the three moments of externalization, objectivation and internalization".[38]

*

If we after this quick survey briefly consider the way in which psychologists, psychiatrists, and sociologists early on employed ideas from phenomenology in their research, it is significant that they often took inspiration from ideas found in Husserl's early descriptive phenomenology. These included Husserl's interest in intentional experience and his insistence on the importance of carefully attending to the phenomena in their full concreteness with the aim of avoiding what Spiegelberg would later call the "premature strait-jacketing of the phenomena by preconceived theories".[39] To insist that the investigation should be conducted in an open-minded manner and be guided by what is given, i.e., by the subject matter at hand, rather than by what we expect to find given our prior theoretical commitments, can certainly be seen as a methodological recommendation. It was in part such recommendations that helped the disciplines in question challenge dominant theories such as behaviourism, positivism, and various forms of reductionism. In addition, many also took inspiration from specific phenomenological concepts such as embodiment, empathy, or the lifeworld. In most cases, the adoption of phenomenological ideas happened in accordance with criteria of usefulness and relevance, rather than by a concern for methodological purity or strict orthodoxy. Schutz is perhaps the most pronounced example of this. As he repeatedly makes clear, his study of the social world doesn't adhere to or employ the strict phenomenological method. Schutz is explicitly interested in a phenomenology conducted from within the natural attitude, i.e., in a non-transcendental phenomenology that can manage without the phenomenological reduction.[40]

NOTES

1 For a comprehensive discussion of this development, see Spiegelberg, H. (1972). *Phenomenology in Psychology and Psychiatry.* Evanston, IL: Northwestern University Press.

2 Husserl, E. (2001b). *Logical Investigations I–II*, trans. J.N. Findlay. London: Routledge: I/6.

3 Husserl, E. (1977). *Phenomenological Psychology: Lectures, Summer Semester, 1925*, trans. J. Scanlon. The Hague: Martinus Nijhoff: 38.

4 Husserl, E. (1997). *Psychological and Transcendental Phenomenology and the Confrontation with Heidegger (1927–1931)*, ed. and trans. T. Sheehan and R.E. Palmer. Dordrecht: Kluwer Academic Publishers: 218–219, 223, 230.

5 Husserl, E. (1970). *The Crisis of European Sciences and Transcendental Phenomenology: An Introduction to Phenomenological Philosophy*, trans. D. Carr. Evanston, IL: Northwestern University Press: 206.

6 Husserl, E. (1997). *Psychological and Transcendental Phenomenology and the Confrontation with Heidegger (1927–1931)*, ed. and trans. T. Sheehan and R.E. Palmer. Dordrecht: Kluwer Academic Publishers: 252.

7 MacLeod, R.B. (1954). David Katz 1884–1953. *Psychological Review* 61(1): 3.

8 Quoted in Spiegelberg, H. (1972). *Phenomenology in Psychology and Psychiatry*. Evanston, IL: Northwestern University Press: 43.

9 Katz, D. (1999). *The World of Colour*, trans. R.B. MacLeod and C.W. Fox. Abingdon: Routledge: 5.

10 Katz, D. (1989). *The World of Touch*, trans. L.E. Krueger. Hillsdale, NJ: Lawrence Erlbaum Associates: 50–53.

11 Katz, D. (1989). *The World of Touch*, trans. L.E. Krueger. Hillsdale, NJ: Lawrence Erlbaum Associates: 76.

12 It has subsequently become customary to speak of the Dutch school in phenomenological psychology (dominated by people such as Buytendijk, Berg, and Linschoten) and the Copenhagen school of phenomenology (represented by Rubin, From, and Tranekjær Rasmussen) (see Kockelmans, J.J. (ed.) (1987). *Phenomenological Psychology: The Dutch School*. Dordrecht: Springer and Hansen, C.R. and Karpatschof, B. (eds.) (2001). *Københavner-fænomenologien, Bisat eller Genfødt?* København: Danmarks Pædagogiske Universitet).

13 Straus, E. (1963). *The Primary World of Senses: A Vindication of Sensory Experience*, trans. J. Needleman. New York, NY: The Free Press of Glencoe; Linschoten, J. (1987). On falling asleep. In J.J. Kockelmans (ed.), *Phenomenological Psychology: The Dutch School* (pp. 79–117). Dordrecht: Springer; From, F. (1953). *Om Oplevelsen af Andres Adfærd: Et Bidrag til den Menneskelige Adfærds Fænomenologi*. København: Nyt Nordisk Forlag.

14 Jaspers, K. (1912). Die phänomenologische forschungsrichtung in der psychopathologie. *Zeitschrift für die gesamte Neurologie und Psychiatrie* 9: 391–408.

15 Laing, R.D. (1963). Minkowski and schizophrenia. *Review of Existential Psychology and Psychiatry* 3(3): 207.

16 Minkowski, E. (2019). *Lived Time: Phenomenological and Psychopathological Studies*, trans. N. Metzel. Evanston, IL: Northwestern University Press: xv.

17 Minkowski, E. (2019). *Lived Time: Phenomenological and Psychopathological Studies*, trans. N. Metzel. Evanston, IL: Northwestern University Press: 185, 222, 228.

18 Minkowski, E. (2019). *Lived Time: Phenomenological and Psychopathological Studies*, trans. N. Metzel. Evanston, IL: Northwestern University Press: 227.

19 Varela, F.J., Thompson, E., and Rosch, E. (1991). *The Embodied Mind: Cognitive Science and Human Experience*. Cambridge, MA: MIT Press: 15; Gallagher, S. (1997). Mutual enlightenment: Recent phenomenology in cognitive science. *Journal of Consciousness Studies* 4(3): 195–214.

20 Minkowski, E. (2019). *Lived Time: Phenomenological and Psychopathological Studies*, trans. N. Metzel. Evanston, IL: Northwestern University Press: xv.

21 Husserl, E. (1962). *Phänomenologische Psychologie. Vorlesungen Sommersemester 1925*, ed. by W. Biemel. Husserliana 9. The Hague: Martinus Nijhoff: 539.

22 Schutz, A. (1962). *The Problem of Social Reality: Collected Papers I*. The Hague: Martinus Nijhoff: 34–35; Schutz, A. (1964). *Studies in Social Theory: Collected Papers II*. The Hague: Martinus Nijhoff: 6–7.

23 Schutz, A. (1964). *Studies in Social Theory: Collected Papers II*. The Hague: Martinus Nijhoff: 250, 252

24 Schutz, A. (1967). *The Phenomenology of the Social World*, trans. G. Walsh and F. Lehnert. Evanston, IL: Northwestern University Press: 14.

25 Schutz, A. (1967). *The Phenomenology of the Social World*, trans. G. Walsh and F. Lehnert. Evanston, IL: Northwestern University Press: 181, 184.

26 Schutz, A. (1962). *The Problem of Social Reality: Collected Papers I*. The Hague: Martinus Nijhoff: 17.

27 Schutz, A. (1962). *The Problem of Social Reality: Collected Papers I*. The Hague: Martinus Nijhoff: 25–26.

28 Schutz, A. (1962). *The Problem of Social Reality: Collected Papers I*. The Hague: Martinus Nijhoff: 14–15.

29 Schutz, A. (1962). *The Problem of Social Reality: Collected Papers I*. The Hague: Martinus Nijhoff: 15, 149.

30 Schutz, A. (1964). *Studies in Social Theory: Collected Papers II*. The Hague: Martinus Nijhoff: 122–123.

31 Berger, P.L. and Luckmann, T. (1991). *The Social Construction of Reality: A Treatise in the Sociology of Knowledge*. Harmondsworth: Penguin Books: 15.

32 Berger, P.L. and Luckmann, T. (1991). *The Social Construction of Reality: A Treatise in the Sociology of Knowledge*. Harmondsworth: Penguin Books: 27.

33 Berger, P.L. and Luckmann, T. (1991). *The Social Construction of Reality: A Treatise in the Sociology of Knowledge*. Harmondsworth: Penguin Books: 106.

34 Berger, P.L. and Luckmann, T. (1991). *The Social Construction of Reality: A Treatise in the Sociology of Knowledge*. Harmondsworth: Penguin Books: 70.

35 Berger, P.L. and Luckmann, T. (1991). *The Social Construction of Reality: A Treatise in the Sociology of Knowledge*. Harmondsworth: Penguin Books: 85–96.

36 Berger, P.L. and Luckmann, T. (1991). *The Social Construction of Reality: A Treatise in the Sociology of Knowledge*. Harmondsworth: Penguin Books: 78.

37 Berger, P.L. and Luckmann, T. (1991). *The Social Construction of Reality: A Treatise in the Sociology of Knowledge*. Harmondsworth: Penguin Books: 149–157.

38 Berger, P.L. and Luckmann, T. (1991). *The Social Construction of Reality: A Treatise in the Sociology of Knowledge*. Harmondsworth: Penguin Books: 149.

39 Spiegelberg, H. (1972). *Phenomenology in Psychology and Psychiatry*. Evanston, IL: Northwestern University Press: 308.

40 Schutz, A. (1962). *The Problem of Social Reality: Collected Papers I.* The Hague: Martinus Nijhoff: 136–137, 149; Schutz, A. (1967). *The Phenomenology of the Social World*, trans. G. Walsh and F. Lehnert. Evanston, IL: Northwestern University Press: 44, 97.

SUGGESTIONS FOR FURTHER READING

Peter L. Berger and Thomas Luckmann, *The Social Construction of Reality: A Treatise in the Sociology of Knowledge*. Harmondsworth: Penguin, 1991.

Herbert Spiegelberg, *Phenomenology in Psychology and Psychiatry*. Evanston, IL: Northwestern University Press, 1972.

Joseph J. Kockelmans (ed.), *Phenomenological Psychology: The Dutch School*. Dordrecht: Martinus Nijhoff, 1987.

Giovanni Stanghellini et al. (eds.), *The Oxford Handbook of Phenomenological Psychopathology*. Oxford: Oxford University Press, 2019.

CURRENT DEBATES IN QUALITATIVE RESEARCH AND THE COGNITIVE SCIENCES

Much of the seminal work in phenomenological psychology, psychiatry, and sociology took place in the 1920s and 1930s. Let us now more forward in time and consider recent work on phenomenology as a qualitative research method.

QUALITATIVE RESEARCH

Qualitative research methods are widely used in disciplines such as sociology, psychology, and anthropology to obtain rich and nuanced descriptions of how people experience and understand themselves and the social world they live in. Given such aims, it is not that surprising that some have taken phenomenology to offer important guidelines for how to conduct qualitative research. Let me briefly present and compare three of the most popular and influential proposals, namely 1) Amedeo Giorgi's *descriptive phenomenological method*, 2) Jonathan Smith's *interpretative phenomenological analysis* (IPA), and 3) Max van Manen's *hermeneutic phenomenology*.[1] All three enjoy wide popularity and are routinely referenced and used by qualitative researchers. As we shall see, all three differ in their methodological recommendations and in how they apply phenomenology. Should phenomenological qualitative research remain purely descriptive and

DOI: 10.4324/9781003350682-15

seek to disclose essential structures, or should it rather focus on the particularity of individual persons and employ interpretation? Should it embrace and adopt part of Husserl's philosophical methodology, or should it rather let its research be guided by various phenomenological concepts and distinctions?

1. Amedeo Giorgi's approach is very explicit about its Husserlian orientation and background, and Giorgi has specifically argued that his own phenomenological psychology involves an adaptation and modification of the philosophical method originally developed by Husserl.[2] The overarching aim of Giorgi's approach is to offer a faithful description of the essential structures of lived experience. To achieve this goal, three methodological steps are often highlighted. The first and most important one concerns the explicit use of the *phenomenological reduction*. As Giorgi insists, scientific research cannot claim phenomenological status unless it is supported by some use of the reduction.[3] More specifically, Giorgi argues that it is essential that the researcher assumes the

> attitude of the phenomenological reduction which means that she must resist from positing as existing whatever object or state of affairs is present to her. The researcher still considers what is given to her but she treats it as something that is present to her consciousness and she refrains from saying that it actually is the way it presents itself to her.[4]

In short, one should not assume that whatever one experiences or is being informed about by others actually does exist or did occur, rather one should simply focus on it as given, as a presence to be explored. Secondly, phenomenological psychology must be *descriptive*, rather than interpretative or explanatory.[5] The psychologist should describe how the given is experienced by the experiencer, and this should be done without adding to or subtracting from what is given.[6] One should avoid interpreting the given with the help of prior theoretical presuppositions, and instead cultivate a heightened awareness of what is actually present. Finally, the knowledge one should aim for should be general and systematic. On the basis of a careful examination of concrete examples, one should seek to extract invariant structures. For Giorgi, the method of phenomenological psychology consequently involves three steps: 1) the phenomenological reduction, 2) the descriptive focus, and 3) the search for essences.[7]

In terms of more practical guidelines, Giorgi has advocated a multi-step procedure that the researcher should use when analysing the descriptions she has collected from the participants. The researcher should first read the entire interview transcript in order to get a sense of its overall meaning. At this stage, no analysis should take place. The next step is to divide the description into smaller meaning units. For each of these meaning units, the researcher should then seek to discover, articulate, and explicate its psychological value and significance. In a final step, the researcher should synthesise the different findings in order to capture the essence of the experience under investigation.[8] Whereas Giorgi provides very detailed instructions regarding the analysis of the transcribed interview, he has less to say about how the interview itself is to be conducted. He does note, however, that one should let the participant speak, as long as she is speaking about her experience. If she starts to drift away, and instead begins to theorise about the experience, the interviewer should gently steer the participant back to the description.[9] As Giorgi writes, the phenomenological researcher "does not care what the specific details or contents are, only that they are genuinely revelatory of the experience being researched".[10] In a subsequent application of Giorgi's method, we find Beck explaining that the interviewed participants should be asked to offer descriptions of their experiences, and that follow-up questions should only be used if "certain parts of the description seemed to be lacking clarity or depth".[11] Statements like these suggest that the interviewer is assigned a somewhat passive role in the process.

2. In recent years, Smith's *interpretative phenomenological analysis* (IPA) has gained increasing popularity among qualitative researchers. The focus of this method is idiographic in that it seeks to understand how particular events and life episodes are experienced by particular individuals. What is it like for John to live with severe mental illness? How does George experience being homeless? How is Anne's sense of her own identity changed as a result of becoming a mother? IPA is, consequently, not interested in essential structures, but in offering detailed explorations and microanalyses of concrete cases.[12] Furthermore, unlike Giorgi, Smith is not primarily drawing on Husserlian

phenomenology, but rather on a wider range of phenomenological authors. He makes no appeal to the phenomenological reduction and takes issue with the idea that a phenomenological psychology must remain purely descriptive. Smith holds that we, as human beings, are always already engaged in interpretative meaning-making activities. Interpretation is a basic structure of our intentional life and consequently not only permissible, but unavoidable.[13]

The approach of IPA is clearly qualitative. It is non-reductive and it seeks to provide rich experiential descriptions. But is that enough to secure its phenomenological credentials? In one of his early texts on the topic, Smith explains that he chose the term "interpretative phenomenological analysis" for his own approach, since his aim was to "explore the participant's view of the world and to adopt, as far as is possible, an 'insider's perspective' of the phenomenon under study".[14] Smith also writes that IPA is a phenomenological approach

> in that it involves detailed examination of the participant's lifeworld; it attempts to explore personal experience and is concerned with an individual's personal perception or account of an object or event, as opposed to an attempt to produce an objective statement of the object or event itself.[15]

One question to ask, however, is whether it really is sufficient to simply consider the perspective of the agent/patient/client in order to qualify the approach as phenomenological? Phenomenologically informed qualitative research has different aims than phenomenological philosophy, but can the former really qualify as phenomenological if it doesn't engage at all with the latter? One popular introduction to IPA, *Interpretative Phenomenological Analysis: Theory, Method and Research*, does contain brief descriptions of the theoretical work of Husserl, Heidegger, Merleau-Ponty, and Sartre, but it remains rather unclear what role their work actually plays in the subsequent description of the method.[16]

In a heated exchange between Smith and van Manen in *Qualitative Health Research*, van Manen accused Smith of hijacking the term "phenomenology" for his own type of psychological analysis,[17] and argued that Smith's framework was "hopelessly misrepresentative of phenomenology in any acceptable sense".[18] In his reply, Smith warned against being overly prescriptive about what counts as phenomenological and insisted that no single person has the authority to prescribe rules about what does or does not constitute phenomenology.[19] This might be right, but it would be unwise to simply accept the flipside of this and embrace any definition. By labelling itself the way it does, IPA clearly wants to stress the link between its own endeavour and the tradition of phenomenological philosophy. It is not obvious, however, that that link amounts to very much, and it is hard to disagree with Giorgi when he writes that it would have been better if IPA had instead been termed IEA: Interpretative experiential analysis.[20]

3. A recurrent claim of van Manen is that qualitative researchers should not make do with secondary literature, but must return to the origin and consult "the primary literature, tradition, and movements of phenomenology".[21] Like Giorgi, van Manen consequently argues that qualitative researchers interested in phenomenology must have some knowledge of its theoretical underpinnings and implications.[22] Based on his own engagement with the writings of a whole range of influential figures in classical and contemporary phenomenological philosophy, van Manen has made some specific claims concerning (a) the aim of a phenomenological investigation and (b) the nature of the phenomenological method.

When it comes to the aim, van Manen claims that phenomenology is the study of the lived meaning of experience. Indeed, van Manen claims that the basic phenomenological question is the question of "What is that experience like?",[23] and he mentions questions such as "What is it like to sip coffee?" and "What is it like to share the experience of looking at water from a bridge?"[24] as examples of core phenomenological questions. When van Manen also claims that phenomenology is the "pursuit of insight into the phenomenality of lived experience"[25] and that Husserlian phenomenology is not concerned with the external object, but only with our experience of that object,[26] it should be clear that he is departing markedly from the account of phenomenology I have offered in previous chapters. As already mentioned, the focus of phenomenology is on the intersection between mind and world, neither of which can be understood in separation from each other. To speak more concretely, a phenomenological investigation of a perceptual experience or an experience of fear must also investigate the intentional correlate, the perceived or feared object. To suggest that only the former is within the purview of phenomenology is to misunderstand Husserl's project.

Ultimately, van Manen is not giving us the original sense of phenomenology but unwittingly propagating an understanding of phenomenology that can also be found in analytic philosophy of mind. In the latter field, there is currently a widespread recognition of the fact that a proper account of consciousness must include and address phenomenology, but the term "phenomenology" is frequently simply used as a synonym for "phenomenality", that is, as a label for the qualitative character of experience. To discuss phenomenology in that context is consequently to discuss a certain dimension of experience and at best to offer first-person descriptions of what the "what it is like" of experience is really like. This way of talking about phenomenology has, however, little to do with phenomenology understood as a distinct philosophical project.

What about the method? While occasionally insisting that "the method of phenomenology is that there is no method", van Manen has also claimed that phenomenology is a tradition that provides "a methodological ground for present human science research practices"[27] and spoken of the need to employ the basic method of phenomenological analysis, namely "the epoché and the reduction", if one is to disclose "the phenomenological meaning of a human experience".[28]

We find similar methodological recommendations in van Manen's acclaimed book *Phenomenology of Practice*, where he also quite reasonably stresses the importance of not presenting the project and methodology of phenomenology in an overly technical manner. Indeed, a central aim of the book has been to make "phenomenological philosophy accessible and do-able by researchers who are not themselves professional philosophers or who do not possess an extensive and in-depth background in the relevant phenomenological philosophical literature".[29] In the chapter specifically discussing the method of philosophical phenomenology, however, van Manen doesn't merely refer to the epoché and the reduction, but introduces the reader to the heuristic reduction, the hermeneutic reduction, the experiential reduction, the methodological reduction, the eidetic reduction, the ontological reduction, the ethical reduction, the radical reduction, and the originary reduction.[30] This is neither a non-technical and easily accessible presentation of philosophical phenomenology, nor is it solidly rooted in and based on the original texts, since many of the terms are van Manen's own inventions.

★

The approaches of Giorgi, Smith, and van Manen have been tremendously influential, but are they exemplary? From time to time, critical voices have expressed reservations about the methodological rigour of these approaches. One persistent critic is John Paley, who for years has attempted to convince qualitative researchers that they shouldn't look to phenomenology if they are on the lookout for philosophical inspiration or methodological guidance.[31]

In his most comprehensive discussion, the book *Phenomenology as Qualitative Research*, Paley argues that a critical assessment of phenomenology as a qualitative research method should be conducted without engaging at all with phenomenological philosophy, since the "convolutions" of the latter "can only be a distraction".[32] Indeed, on his account, Husserl "can be almost wilfully obscure".[33] This is hardly a promising setup, and it shouldn't surprise that the conclusion Paley eventually reaches is quite unfavourable. After an extensive discussion of Giorgi, Smith, and van Manen, Paley claims that all three fail to provide clear definitions of the central concepts they use and that their approaches lack methodological rigour, employ arbitrary procedures, and are thoroughly permeated by personal idiosyncrasies.[34] Paley's work has subsequently been applauded for having revealed the "emperor's lack of clothing and pushed him into the spotlight for all to see".[35] It has even led some to ask the question, "Is there nursing phenomenology after Paley?"[36]

It would lead us too far afield to offer a more comprehensive assessment of Paley's rather uncharitable criticism here,[37] but it is noteworthy that he remains so focused on criticising Giorgi, Smith, and van Manen that he completely overlooks the existence of other approaches and resources. Not only have there in recent years been efforts to develop new ways of adopting and applying phenomenological ideas in qualitative research,[38] but these efforts have also partially been inspired by a parallel development that for more than three decades has sought to apply ideas from phenomenology in the domain of the cognitive sciences.

THE COGNITIVE SCIENCES

Is it possible to bridge the gap between phenomenological analyses and empirical work on consciousness? Although the question has been discussed since the beginning of the 20th century, there is no doubt that the work of the Chilean neuroscientist Francisco Varela (1946–2001) rekindled interest in the question.

In a number of publications up through the 1990s, Varela outlined a novel approach in cognitive neuroscience, one which considered the data from phenomenologically disciplined analyses of lived experience and the experimentally based accounts found in cognitive neuroscience to have equal status and to be linked by mutual constraints.[39] As Varela pointed out, if the cognitive sciences are to accomplish their goal, namely to provide a truly scientific theory of consciousness, they cannot and must not ignore the experiential dimension, since they would thereby be disregarding a crucial part of the explanandum. To put it differently, if our aim is to obtain a comprehensive understanding of the mind, then focusing narrowly on the nature of the subpersonal events that underlie experience without considering the qualities and structures of the experience itself will just not take us very far. More specifically, Varela argued that the subjective dimension is intrinsically open to intersubjective validation, if only we avail ourselves of a method and procedure for doing so. He thought classical philosophical phenomenology had provided such a method and considered it crucial for the future development of the cognitive sciences that cognitive scientists actually learned to use some of the methodological tools that had been developed by Husserl and Merleau-Ponty.[40]

The inspiration from Merleau-Ponty is particularly evident. Already in his first published work *The Structure of Behavior* from 1942, we find Merleau-Ponty engaging with the work of psychologists such as Freud, Pavlov, Koffka, Watson, Wallon, and Piaget. The last section of the book carries the heading "Is there not a truth in naturalism?" This interest in empirical research, in its importance for phenomenology, remained prominent in many of Merleau-

Ponty's later works. His reference to and use of neuropathology (Gelb and Goldstein's analysis of the brain-damaged patient Schneider) in *Phenomenology of Perception* is particularly striking. For some years, in the period 1949–1952, Merleau-Ponty even taught developmental psychology at Sorbonne. Throughout, Merleau-Ponty didn't conceive of the relation between phenomenology and empirical science as a question of how to simply apply already obtained phenomenological insights. Merleau-Ponty's view was rather that both sides could profit from and flourish as a result of their dialogue and exchange.

Heralding Merleau-Ponty as someone who already early on "argued for the mutual illumination among a phenomenology of direct lived experience, psychology and neurophysiology",[41] one of Varela's more specific proposals was that one should incorporate phenomenological forms of investigation into the experimental protocols of neuroscientific research on consciousness. One should train the participating subjects to set aside their preconceived ideas and theories and teach them to focus their attention on the experience itself in order to bring into focus dimensions and aspects of consciousness that normally remain unnoticed. Subsequently, one should then ask them to provide careful descriptions of these experiences using an open-question format. The ensuing descriptions could subsequently be validated intersubjectively, and then be used in the analysis and interpretation of the correlated neurophysiological processes.[42]

Varela's initial publications in this area generated an intense debate about the relation between phenomenology and the cognitive sciences, and more generally about whether phenomenology could and ought to be naturalised.[43] Not surprisingly, one issue of controversy was the question of what precisely such a naturalisation might imply.

One answer can be found in the long introduction to the milestone work *Naturalizing Phenomenology* from 1999, which Varela co-edited. In the introduction, the four editors argued that the ultimate goal must be a natural explanation of consciousness, i.e., an explanation that only appeals to entities and properties admitted by the natural sciences, and that this will require phenomenology to be integrated into the explanatory framework of natural science.[44]

According to this proposal, to naturalise phenomenology entails making phenomenology into a part of, or at least an extension of, natural science. At the same time, however, the editors also spoke of the need for recasting the very notion of nature and objectivity and claimed that it was necessary to dispense with the idea that scientific objectivity presupposes a commitment to an observer-independent reality.[45]

According to a rather different proposal, to naturalise phenomenology simply means to let phenomenology be informed by and engage with empirical research. What form should this engagement take? In an article from 2000 entitled "Bridging embodied cognition and brain function: The role of phenomenology", Borrett, Kelly, and Kwan argued as follows:

> [T]he right relation between phenomenology and brain science is that of data to model: brain science is ultimately concerned with explaining the way the physical processes of the brain conspire to produce the phenomena of human experience; insofar as phenomenology devotes itself to the accurate description of these phenomena, it provides the most complete and accurate presentation of the data that ultimately must be accounted for by models of brain function [. . .]. Thus, the phenomenological account of a given aspect of human behavior is meant to provide a description of the characteristics of that behavior which any physical explanation of it must be able to reproduce.[46]

This suggestion is far too modest, however. Phenomenology does offer detailed analyses of perception, imagination, body-awareness, recollection, social cognition, self-experience, temporality, etc., and in providing such analyses, phenomenology can do more than merely supply data to existing models, can provide more than refined descriptions of an already established explanandum. Phenomenology is not merely in the descriptive business. It also offers theoretical accounts of its own that can challenge existing models and background assumptions, and which might occasionally lead to the discovery of quite different explananda. At the same time, however, insofar as phenomenology studies phenomena that are open to empirical investigation, it ought to be informed by the best available scientific knowledge, and in some cases empirical findings might challenge the classical phenomenological analyses and thereby also lead to a revision or refinement of them. The phenomenological slogan "Back to the things themselves" calls for us to let our experience guide our theories. We should pay attention to the way in which reality is experientially manifest. Empirical researchers might not pay much attention to deep philosophical questions, but as empirical researchers they do in fact pay quite a lot of attention to concrete phenomena and might consequently be less apt than the average armchair philosopher to underestimate the richness, complexity, and variety of the phenomena.

Let me offer some concrete examples that can illustrate what in the best instance might be called relations of mutual enlightenment.

1 In Chapter 7, I presented various facets of the phenomenological analyses of embodiment. We saw how phenomenologists in different ways highlighted the crucial importance of pre-reflective body-awareness. Recent literature on neuropathology offers rich descriptions of various disorders of this tacit body-awareness, which have subsequently been taken up and discussed by researchers influenced by phenomenology. Consider, for example, Jonathan Cole's careful analysis of Ian Waterman, who at the age of 19, due to illness, lost all sense of touch and proprioception from the neck down.[47] When Waterman shortly after the onset of his disorder, tried to move a limb or his entire body, he could initiate the movement, but had no control over where the moving part ended up. If he reached for something, the hands would miss or overshoot wildly, and unless he kept an eye on his hands, they would start to "wander", and he would only be able to relocate them by means of vision. It was only after an intensely difficult learning process that he was able to regain some control over his movements. But his awareness of his body was transformed. His previous pre-reflective awareness of bodily movements was no longer operative and available and had been replaced by a reflective body-awareness. Every single movement required intense mental concentration and visual monitoring. Even to sit in a chair without falling out of it required constant attention. When standing, Waterman could also easily fall over if he closed his eyes, if the light went out, or if he sneezed. Over

time, Waterman became more adept at walking, not because attention was no longer required, but because the deliberate control became less taxing as a result of constant practice.[48] On the one hand, this case study demonstrates how dependent our ability to act is on our pre-reflective body-awareness, and how dramatically disabling an impairment of the latter is. To that extent, the case might serve as a good illustration of the empirical relevance of some of the phenomenological distinctions and analyses. On the other hand, however, the case of Waterman might also force us to revisit some of the classical phenomenological accounts. Despite his almost complete lack of proprioception, Waterman was to some extent able to regain control over and re-appropriate his body. This suggests not only that we might be more resilient than assumed, but also that compensatory strategies are available that the classical phenomenologists might not have foreseen.

2 The second example comes from the domain of developmental psychology. In Chapter 8, we saw how phenomenologists have criticised the suggestion that interpersonal understanding is at its core a theory-driven inferential process, and how they instead favoured an embodied perceptual approach to the problem of intersubjectivity. Their account of the latter has been corroborated and refined by a number of developmental psychologists, who have investigated fundamental but primitive forms of social understanding found in infants and young children.[49] Whereas we, in adult life, regularly make inferential attributions of mental states to other people, such attributions cannot be considered the basis of the smooth and immediate interpersonal interaction – often called primary intersubjectivity – found in young infants.[50] From very early on, infants are able to discriminate animate and inanimate objects and distinguish biological movement from non-biological movement. In an article surveying and summarising research on socio-cognitive development in infancy, Rochat and Striano concluded that infants manifest an essentially innate sensitivity to social stimuli, that there is an early form of intersubjectivity at play from around two months of age, where the infant has a sense of shared experience and reciprocity with others,[51] and that the "echoing of affects, feelings and emotions that

takes place in reciprocal interaction between young infants and their caretakers" is a "necessary element to the development of more advanced social cognition, including theory of mind".[52] Two- to three-month-old infants will already engage in "proto-conversations" with other people by smiling and vocalising, and will demonstrate a capacity to vary the timing and intensity of communication with their partners. In fact, infants seem to expect people to communicate reciprocally with them in face-to-face interactions and will work actively to sustain and regulate the interaction. Findings in developmental psychology can not only corroborate central claims found in phenomenological work on, say, empathy,[53] they also offer far more detailed descriptions of a range of specific social phenomena. Finally, they can challenge some of the claims made by phenomenologists. Drawing on the empirical research of his time, Merleau-Ponty, for instance, argued that there is no self–other differentiation at birth and that infants only start to perceive others at around six months of age.[54] These are claims that subsequent empirical research has called into question.[55]

3 As a final example, let us consider the case of psychopathology. The tradition of phenomenological psychiatry did not end with Minkowski, but has continued to flourish and is currently represented by figures like Josef Parnas, Louis Sass, and Thomas Fuchs. All of these authors have been inspired by phenomenological work on self and self-experience, especially the idea that experience by virtue of its subjective or first-personal character necessarily involves a fundamental form of for-me-ness.[56] It has been argued that schizophrenia involves transformations and alterations of this very basic sense of self and that such self-disorders may be ascribed a generating, pathogenic role. They antecede, underlie, and shape the emergence of later and psychotic pathology and may thus unify what, from a purely descriptive psychiatric standpoint, may seem to be unrelated or even antithetical syndromes and symptoms.[57] At the same time, this empirical work on anomalous self-experience and alienated forms of self-consciousness has not only allowed for further refinements of the phenomenological understanding of selfhood,[58] but has also been taken up in clinical practice.

A milestone event in this development was the publication in 2005 of a qualitative semi-structured psychometric checklist containing 57 different items called EASE (*Examination of Anomalous Self-Experience*). The checklist, which drew on many years of clinical work and was inspired and informed by ideas found in philosophical phenomenology, was precisely designed to support a systematic exploration and assessment of subtle disturbances of subjective experiences.[59] Subsequent results indicate that the presence of anomalous subjective experiences, in particular self-disorders and perplexity, are important prognostic indicators and can help to identify those with a high risk of developing schizophrenia.[60]

One issue highlighted by EASE concerns the nature of the phenomenological interview. How are such interviews to be conducted? As we have already seen, one idea occasionally defended by qualitative researchers is that one has to be very careful in not asking any guiding questions. If the aim is to understand how particular events and life episodes are experienced by the individuals in question, it is important to allow the interviewees to express themselves about their own experience without being unduly influenced or constrained by the interviewer's research agenda. This is why Wood, for instance, even suggests that "in true phenomenological research only one question is usually asked to elicit data".[61] Typically, the opening question will be quite broad and non-directive, and simply be a question that encourages the interviewee to start describing his or her experiences. However, such an approach is confronted with a fairly obvious problem. What if the participants who are being interviewed and who are requested to provide rich descriptions of, say, what it is like to live with schizophrenia or diabetes, are only able to offer very coarse and superficial descriptions?

EASE exemplifies a very different approach. Rather than simply assuming that the interviewee is able to come up with rich descriptions from the outset and that the task of the interviewer is merely to register everything being said, the idea is rather to engage collaboratively with the interviewee in order to co-generate knowledge. In short, the task of the interviewer is to engage in a kind of Socratic midwifery and help the interviewee obtain new insights of his or her own. To allow for this collaboration, the interviewer 1) must adopt an open-minded and empathic attitude in order to establish basic trust with the interviewee, 2) must engage in a continuous self-critical assessment of his or her own preconceptions and biases, and, 3) must engage pro-actively with the interviewee in order to elicit relevantly detailed descriptions.[62] Using the checklist provided by the EASE manual, the psychiatrists engage exploratively with the participants and conduct semi-structured interviews in order to elicit descriptions regarding various domains that are considered to be of particular relevance. This might, for instance, include bodily, temporal, and social dimensions, i.e., dimensions the significance of which have precisely been highlighted by phenomenological philosophers. Although one should of course be prepared to revise one's theoretical assumptions in the face of what the patient is saying, a methodological prerequisite for doing the interview is by no means that one initially strips one's own mind of preconceived ideas. On the contrary, it is all about conducting the interview in light of quite specific ideas and notions that derive from phenomenological theory. The phenomenological character of this approach is consequently not simply to be found in its interest in eliciting first-person reports from the patients. It is very much about also employing a comprehensive theoretical framework concerning the structure of the subject's relation to itself, to the world, and to others that will allow one to ask the right kind of questions.

It is noteworthy that patients interviewed on the basis of EASE often express feelings of relief when realizing that the interviewer is familiar with the nature of their experiences and that others suffer from similar experiences. This in itself can make the experiences less frightening and disturbing. The very fact of being listened to and taken seriously consequently has therapeutic value, and often patients who have been in treatment for years wonder why nobody has ever asked them these types of questions before.

The attempt to employ ideas from phenomenology in the empirical study of the mind remains controversial in the eyes of many advocates of mainstream cognitive science. Although many might now be prepared to concede that a scientific investigation of consciousness should also consider and address the experiential side of matters – and that a non-technical sense of phenomenology might, consequently, be relevant – the majority would resist the suggestion that they ought to accept or embrace any of the more specific methodological procedures or theoretical assumptions found in classical philosophical phenomenology. Nevertheless, the work of Varela, Thompson, Gallagher, and others have triggered an intense and ongoing debate. It led to the launch of the journal *Phenomenology and the Cognitive Sciences* and has also proven influential in the continuing development of other related areas including research on embodied cognition and sense-making.

NOTES

1 For a discussion that also covers several additional approaches, see Finlay, L. (2009). Debating phenomenological research methods. *Phenomenology & Practice* 3(1): 6–25.

2 Giorgi, A. (2009). *The Descriptive Phenomenological Method in Psychology: A Modified Husserlian Approach.* Pittsburgh, PA: Duquesne University Press: 104.

3 Giorgi, A. (2010). Phenomenology and the practice of science. *Existential Analysis* 21(1): 18.

4 Giorgi, A. (2012). The descriptive phenomenological psychological method. *Journal of Phenomenological Psychology* 43(1): 4.

5 Giorgi, A. (2009). *The Descriptive Phenomenological Method in Psychology: A Modified Husserlian Approach.* Pittsburgh, PA: Duquesne University Press: 116.

6 Giorgi, A. (2009). *The Descriptive Phenomenological Method in Psychology: A Modified Husserlian Approach.* Pittsburgh, PA: Duquesne University Press: 9.

7 Giorgi, A. (1994). A phenomenological perspective on certain qualitative research methods. *Journal of Phenomenological Psychology* 25(2): 206.

8 Giorgi, A. (2009). *The Descriptive Phenomenological Method in Psychology: A Modified Husserlian Approach.* Pittsburgh, PA: Duquesne University Press: 128–137.

9 Giorgi, A. (2009). *The Descriptive Phenomenological Method in Psychology: A Modified Husserlian Approach.* Pittsburgh, PA: Duquesne University Press: 122.

10 Giorgi, A. (2009). *The Descriptive Phenomenological Method in Psychology: A Modified Husserlian Approach.* Pittsburgh, PA: Duquesne University Press: 123.

11 Beck, T.J. (2013). A phenomenological analysis of anxiety as experienced in social situations. *Journal of Phenomenological Psychology* 44(2): 188–189.

12 Smith, J.A., Flowers, P., and Larkin, M. (2009). *Interpretative Phenomenological Analysis: Theory, Method and Research*. London: Sage: 16, 202.

13 Smith, J.A., Flowers, P., and Larkin, M. (2009). *Interpretative Phenomenological Analysis: Theory, Method and Research*. London: Sage: 3.

14 Smith, J.A. (1996). Beyond the divide between cognition and discourse: Using interpretative phenomenological analysis in health psychology. *Psychology & Health* 11(2): 264.

15 Smith, J.A. and Osborn, M. (2008). Interpretative phenomenological analysis. In J.A. Smith (ed.), *Qualitative Psychology: A Practical Guide to Research Methods* (pp. 53–80). London: Sage: 53.

16 Smith, J.A., Flowers, P., and Larkin, M. (2009). *Interpretative Phenomenological Analysis: Theory, Method and Research*. London: Sage.

17 van Manen, M. (2017a). But is it phenomenology? *Qualitative Health Research* 27: 778.

18 van Manen, M. (2018). Rebuttal rejoinder: Present IPA for what it is— Interpretative psychological analysis. *Qualitative Health Research* 28: 1962.

19 Smith, J.A. (2018). "Yes it is phenomenological": A reply to Max van Manen's critique of interpretative phenomenological analysis. *Qualitative Health Research* 28: 1955–1958.

20 Giorgi, A. (2010). Phenomenology and the practice of science. *Existential Analysis* 21(1): 6.

21 van Manen, M. (2018). Rebuttal rejoinder: Present IPA for what it is— Interpretative psychological analysis. *Qualitative Health Research* 28: 1966.

22 van Manen, M. (1990). *Researching Lived Experience: Human Science for an Action Sensitive Pedagogy*. London and Ontario: Althouse Press: 8.

23 van Manen, M. (2014). *Phenomenology of Practice: Meaning-giving Methods in Phenomenological Research and Writing*. Walnut Creek, CA: Left Coast Press: 35; van Manen, M. (2017b). Phenomenology it its original sense. *Qualitative Health Research* 27: 811.

24 van Manen, M. (2014). *Phenomenology of Practice: Meaning-giving Methods in Phenomenological Research and Writing*. Walnut Creek, CA: Left Coast Press: 35.

25 van Manen, M. (2017a). But is it phenomenology? *Qualitative Health Research* 27: 779.

26 van Manen, M. (2014). *Phenomenology of Practice: Meaning-giving Methods in Phenomenological Research and Writing*. Walnut Creek, CA: Left Coast Press: 91.

27 van Manen, M. (1990). *Researching Lived Experience: Human Science for an Action Sensitive Pedagogy*. London and Ontario: Althouse Press: 30.

28 van Manen, M. (2017b). Phenomenology it its original sense. *Qualitative Health Research* 27: 820.

29 van Manen, M. (2014). *Phenomenology of Practice: Meaning-giving Methods in Phenomenological Research and Writing*. Walnut Creek, CA: Left Coast Press: 18.

30 van Manen, M. (2014). *Phenomenology of Practice: Meaning-giving Methods in Phenomenological Research and Writing*. Walnut Creek, CA: Left Coast Press: 222.

31 Paley, J. (1997). Husserl, phenomenology and nursing. *Journal of Advanced Nursing* 26(1): 187–193; Paley, J. (2005). Phenomenology as rhetoric. *Nursing Inquiry* 12(2): 106–116; Paley, J. (2017). *Phenomenology as Qualitative Research: A Critical Analysis of Meaning Attribution*. London: Routledge.

32 Paley, J. (2017). *Phenomenology as Qualitative Research: A Critical Analysis of Meaning Attribution*. London: Routledge: 3.

33 Paley, J. (2017). *Phenomenology as Qualitative Research: A Critical Analysis of Meaning Attribution*. London: Routledge: 7.

34 Paley, J. (2017). *Phenomenology as Qualitative Research: A Critical Analysis of Meaning Attribution*. London: Routledge: 28, 147.

35 Watson, R. (2017). Phenomenology as qualitative research: A critical analysis of meaning attribution John Paley (2016), Routledge, ISBN-13: 978-1138652811. *Nursing Philosophy* 18(4): e12180.

36 Petrovskaya, O. (2014), Nursing phenomenology after Paley. *Nursing Philosophy* 15: 60–71.

37 For some replies, see Giorgi, A. (2017). Review essay: A response to the attempted critique of the scientific phenomenological method. *Journal of Phenomenological Psychology* 48(1): 83–144 and van Manen, M. (2017c). Phenomenology and meaning attribution. *Indo-Pacific Journal of Phenomenology* 17(1): 1–12.

38 For recent contributions, see: Høffding, S. and Martiny, K. (2016). Framing a phenomenological interview: What, why and how. *Phenomenology and the Cognitive Sciences* 15(4): 539–564; Heimann, K., Høffding, S., and Martiny, K. (eds.) (2023). *Phenomenological Interviews: Working with Others' Experiences*. Special Issue of *Phenomenology and the Cognitive Sciences* 22: 1–311; Køster, A. and Fernandez, A.V. (2023). Investigating modes of being in the world: An introduction to phenomenologically grounded qualitative research. *Phenomenology and the Cognitive Sciences* 22(1): 149–169.

39 Varela, F.J. (1996). Neurophenomenology: A methodological remedy for the hard problem. *Journal of Consciousness Studies* 3(4): 330–349.

40 Varela, F.J. (1996). Neurophenomenology: A methodological remedy for the hard problem. *Journal of Consciousness Studies* 3(4): 330–349; Varela, F.J. (1997). The naturalization of phenomenology as the transcendence of nature: Searching for generative mutual constraints. *Alter: Revue de Phénoménologie* 5: 355–381; Petitot, J., Varela, F.J., Pachoud, B., and Roy, J.-M. (eds.) (1999). *Naturalizing Phenomenology*. Stanford, CA: Stanford University Press.

41 Varela, F.J., Thompson, E., and Rosch, E. (1991). *The Embodied Mind: Cognitive Science and Human Experience*. Cambridge, MA: MIT Press: 15.

42 Lutz, A., Lachaux, J.-P., Martinerie, J., and Varela, F.J. (2002). Guiding the study of brain dynamics by using first person data: Synchrony patterns correlate with ongoing conscious states during a simple visual task. *Proceedings of the National Academy of Sciences* 99(3): 1586–1591.

43 See, for instance: Gallagher, S. (1997). Mutual enlightenment: Recent phenomenology in cognitive science. *Journal of Consciousness Studies* 4(3): 195–214; Gallagher, S. (2003). Phenomenology and experimental design: Toward a phenomenologically enlightened experimental science. *Journal of*

Consciousness Studies 10(9–10): 85–99; Lutz, A. and Thompson, E. (2003). Neurophenomenology: Integrating subjective experience and brain dynamics in the neuroscience of consciousness. *Journal of Consciousness Studies* 10(9–10): 31–52; Zahavi, D. (2013). Naturalized phenomenology: A desideratum or a category mistake? *Royal Institute of Philosophy Supplements* 72: 23–42; Thompson, E. (2007). *Mind in Life: Biology, Phenomenology, and the Sciences of Mind.* Cambridge, MA: Harvard University Press; Gallagher, S. and Zahavi, D. (2021). *The Phenomenological Mind.* 3rd edn. London: Routledge.

44 Roy, J.-M., Petitot, J., Pachoud, B., and Varela, F.J. (1999). Beyond the gap: An introduction to naturalizing phenomenology. In J. Petitot, F.J. Varela, B. Pachoud, and J.-M. Roy (eds.), *Naturalizing Phenomenology* (pp. 1–83). Stanford, CA: Stanford University Press: 1–2. For a critical discussion, see Zahavi, D. (2004). Phenomenology and the project of naturalization. *Phenomenology and the Cognitive Sciences* 3(4): 331–347.

45 Roy, J.-M., Petitot, J., Pachoud, B., and Varela, F.J. (1999). Beyond the gap: An introduction to naturalizing phenomenology. In J. Petitot, F.J. Varela, B. Pachoud, and J.-M. Roy (eds.), *Naturalizing Phenomenology* (pp. 1–83). Stanford, CA: Stanford University Press: 54. This latter idea is not discussed in more detail in the joint introduction, but it was later picked up and further developed by Thompson, E. (2007). *Mind in Life: Biology, Phenomenology, and the Sciences of Mind.* Cambridge, MA: Harvard University Press.

46 Borrett, D., Kelly, S., and Kwan, H. (2000). Bridging embodied cognition and brain function: The role of phenomenology. *Philosophical Psychology* 13(2): 261–266.

47 Cole, J.D. (1995). *Pride and a Daily Marathon.* Cambridge, MA: MIT Press.

48 Gallagher, S. and Cole, J. (1995). Body image and body schema in a deafferented subject. *Journal of Mind and Behavior* 16(4): 369–390.

49 Stern, D. (2004). *The Present Moment in Psychotherapy and Everyday Life.* New York, NY: W.W. Norton & Company: 94–96.

50 Trevarthen, C. (1979). Communication and cooperation in early infancy: A description of primary intersubjectivity. In M.M. Bullowa (ed.), *Before Speech: The Beginning of Interpersonal Communication* (pp. 321–347). New York, NY: Cambridge University Press.

51 Rochat, P. and Striano, T. (1999). Social-cognitive development in the first year. In P. Rochat (ed.), *Early Social Cognition: Understanding Others in the First Months of Life* (pp. 3–34). Hillsdale, NJ: Lawrence Erlbaum Associates: 4.

52 Rochat, P. and Striano, T. (1999). Social-cognitive development in the first year. In P. Rochat (ed.), *Early Social Cognition: Understanding Others in the First Months of Life* (pp. 3–34). Hillsdale, NJ: Lawrence Erlbaum Associates: 8.

53 See Zahavi, D. (2014). *Self and Other: Exploring Subjectivity, Empathy, and Shame.* Oxford: Oxford University Press.

54 Merleau-Ponty, M. (1964c). *The Primacy of Perception,* ed. by J.M. Edie. Evanston, IL: Northwestern University Press: 119, 125.

55 Gallagher, S. and Meltzoff, A.N. (1996). The earliest sense of self and others: Merleau-Ponty and recent developmental studies. *Philosophical Psychology* 9(2): 211–233.

56 Zahavi, D. (1999a). *Self-awareness and Alterity: A Phenomenological Investigation*. Evanston, IL: Northwestern University Press; Zahavi, D. (2014). *Self and Other: Exploring Subjectivity, Empathy, and Shame*. Oxford: Oxford University Press.

57 Sass, L.A. and Parnas, J. (2003). Schizophrenia, consciousness, and the self. *Schizophrenia Bulletin* 29(3): 427–444.

58 Henriksen, M.G., Parnas, J., and Zahavi, D. (2019). Thought insertion and disturbed for-me-ness (minimal selfhood) in schizophrenia. *Consciousness and Cognition* 74: 102770.

59 Parnas, J., Møller, P., Kircher, T., Thalbitzer, J., Jansson, L., Handest, P., and Zahavi, D. (2005). EASE: Examination of anomalous self-experience. *Psychopathology* 38(5): 236–258.

60 Nelson, B., Thompson, A., and Yung, A.R. (2013). Not all first-episode psychosis is the same: Preliminary evidence of greater basic self-disturbance in schizophrenia spectrum cases. *Early Intervention in Psychiatry* 7(2): 200–204; Møller, P., Haug, E., Raballo, A., Parnas, J., and Melle, I. (2011). Examination of anomalous self-experience in first-episode psychosis: Interrater reliability. *Psychopathology* 44(6): 386–390.

61 Wood, F.G. (1991). The meaning of caregiving. *Rehabilitation Nursing* 16(4): 196.

62 See also Høffding, S. and Martiny, K. (2016). Framing a phenomenological interview: What, why and how. *Phenomenology and the Cognitive Sciences* 15(4): 539–564.

SUGGESTIONS FOR FURTHER READING

Scott D. Churchill and Frederick J. Wertz, "An introduction to phenomenological research in psychology: Historical, conceptual, and methodological foundations." In K.J. Schneider and J.F. Pierson (eds.), *The Handbook of Humanistic Psychology: Leading Edges in Theory, Research, and Practice* (pp. 275–295). Thousand Oaks, CA: Sage, 2015.

Linda Finlay, "Debating phenomenological research methods." *Phenomenology & Practice* 3(1), 2009, 6–25.

Katrin Heimann, Simon Høffding, and Kristian Martiny (eds.), *Phenomenological Interviews: Working with Others' Experiences*. Special Issue of *Phenomenology and the Cognitive Sciences* 22, 2023, 1–311.

Shaun Gallagher and Dan Zahavi, *The Phenomenological Mind*. 3rd edn. London: Routledge, 2021.

A METHOD, AN ATTITUDE, A THEORETICAL FRAMEWORK

If we once again briefly consider some of the classical figures in psychology and psychiatry who were inspired by phenomenological philosophy, it is noteworthy that few of them seemed interested in Husserl's more specific instructions regarding how to methodologically employ the epoché and the reduction. It is not coincidental that Spiegelberg in the conclusion to his survey *Phenomenology in Psychology and Psychiatry* – which covers and discusses an impressive number of figures – explicitly warns against "an orthodox return to Husserl" and argues that it is urgent to free oneself from some of the technicalities of Husserl's philosophy if a true two-way exchange between psychology and phenomenology is to be possible.[1]

One concrete example of this can be found in the work of the psychiatrist Ludwig Binswanger (1881–1966). In his book *Introduction to the Problems of General Psychology* from 1922, Binswanger argued that Husserl's and Scheler's work couldn't merely help empirical psychology gain a more secure foundation, but that it had also produced a number of results of direct relevance for psychology.[2] One specific example that Binswanger then highlights concerns the nature of interpersonal understanding. As Binswanger points out, phenomenologists have recognised that the way we typically encounter other human beings is as undivided psychophysical unities, i.e., neither as mere bodies nor as pure minds.[3] By stressing the existence of a form of social perception and by thereby having eliminated the need for an appeal to a fundamental form of projection or analogical inference, Binswanger took phenomenology to have offered crucial insights to both psychology and psychiatry.[4] In making this argument, Binswanger wasn't merely anticipating much later developments in cognitive science, he was also doing so without referencing the epoché and the phenomenological reduction.

Some contemporary phenomenological psychologists would find this unacceptable. As we have seen, Giorgi would insist that scientific research cannot claim phenomenological status unless it is supported by some use of the reduction.[5] And as Morley has argued in a discussion of phenomenological qualitative research methodology: "It's always about the epoché".[6]

But what exactly was Husserl's reason for introducing these methodological steps in the first place? As I pointed out in Chapter 3, Husserl introduced the epoché in order to suspend our naïve and unquestioned reliance on the existence of a mind-independent reality, and the aim of the subsequent reduction was then to allow for a systematic investigation of the correlation between mind and world; an investigation that would eventually reveal to what extent the latter depends upon subjectivity. As Husserl remarks in *Crisis*, it is only in this manner that the phenomenologist will then be able to achieve his main goal, namely, to transform "the universal obviousness of the being of the world—for him the greatest of all enigmas—into something intelligible".[7]

The obvious question to ask is whether it really is reasonable to insist that anybody wishing to conduct applied phenomenological research, anybody wishing to use phenomenology in educational research, experimental psychology, nursing research, sports science, anthropology, sociology, literary studies, etc., must "resist from positing as existing whatever object or state of affairs is present"[8] and learn to suspend the general thesis and various deep-seated metaphysical assumptions about the mind-independent status of the world. Not only do I think this proposal is without theoretical justification, I also think it has proven quite counterproductive. Instead of letting researchers engage with the phenomena themselves, it has often led them astray by making them choke on methodological meta-reflections and generated an enormous number of publications where protagonists and antagonists alike struggle with these technical concepts and typically end up misinterpreting them. For a few examples, consider the interpretations of Langdridge and Paley. Whereas Langdridge claims that Husserl through his process of bracketing attempted to "transcend [. . .] the *noetic-noematic* correlation and take a 'God's eye view' on experience",[9] Paley writes that Husserl through the phenomenological reduction tried to "break out of experience (into the realm of pure consciousness)".[10] Neither of these interpretations makes much sense, as anybody familiar with Husserl's work would know. The technical and at times arcane complexity of some of the proposed approaches has not only generated internal confusions and led protagonists of different approaches to criticise each other for having misinterpreted central aspects of phenomenology. It has also motivated persisting external criticisms and led to the accusation that applied phenomenology "has risen to prominence on hot air, i.e., jargon-laced gas that obscures the emptiness of its claims and the arbitrariness of its methods".[11] The end result has been that many potential applicants who were looking for theoretical inspiration or methodological guidance have turned to other more easily comprehensible theoretical frameworks.

Any procedure or approach that is supposed to merit the label *phenomenological* must be familiar with phenomenological theory. This is a necessary requirement. In a non-philosophical context, however, a relevant and creative use of central phenomenological concepts such as lifeworld, intentionality, empathy, pre-reflective experience, horizon, historicity, lived body, etc. might be far more valuable and productive than a strict adherence to and insistence on the performance of the epoché and reduction, precisely because the latter procedures have such an explicit philosophical focus and aim. To be very clear, this is not meant to suggest that non-philosophers should somehow be prohibited from making use of these notions, but I fail to see why their employment should be necessary if a non-philosophical engagement with phenomenology is to be deemed successful.

Let me offer a few final examples of such successful uses, and this time from the domain of health care. If we wish to offer proper care, especially in the case of more chronic and life-changing illnesses – care that the patient will find helpful and meaningful – we shouldn't focus on the symptoms in isolation, but need to understand how the illness in question affects the more general life-situation of the patient. We need to understand how it affects the patient's being-in-the-world, e.g., his or her intentional, temporal, spatial, and social sense-making. And this is precisely where health care professionals can profit from phenomenological investigations of intentionality, embodiment, temporality, empathy, spatiality, etc.

In normal life, our bodily capacities are taken for granted. When riding our bike or brushing our teeth, we seldomly attend to our bodily skills. They remain in the background as something we can count on. The fact that the world is given to us as a world of affordances, i.e., as situations of meaning and circumstances for action, as allowing or preventing specific bodily activities, the fact that the body is operative in every perception and every action, the fact that it constitutes our point of view and our point of departure is not something we normally attend to. But of course, this can quickly change, because of pain, exhaustion, illness, or disability. What was previously taken for granted is suddenly problematised. As Carel writes:

> [C]ases of illness make apparent not only the bodily feeling of confidence, familiarity, and continuity that is disturbed, but also a host of assumptions that hang on it. For example, one's future plans depend on bodily capacities and thus are limited by ill health. One's temporal sense is radically changed by a poor prognosis. One's values and sense of what is important in life are frequently modified in light of illness; bodily limitations impact on one's existence generally.[12]

A person who finds himself bound to a wheelchair doesn't simply undergo a change in motor control. He will also find the environment changed. What used to be an easily accessible storeroom in the basement will now appear as an inaccessible and unusable part of the house. Even if the distance to the top shelf of the cupboard remains the same when measured in centimetres, it is now out of reach. In some cases, illness can also be identity transforming. A professional ballet dancer whose kneecap is broken in a traffic accident might have to struggle with the task of redefining who she is, since the goals and activities that she used to consider identity defining are no longer available. Or consider somebody with locked-in syndrome, who is conscious and cognitively unimpaired, but paralysed and unable to communicate verbally. In such circumstances, the body might well be experienced as an antagonist rather than as (part of) who I am.

These brief remarks only touch the surface of a phenomenological analysis of the body, but should make it evident how a familiarity with phenomenological theorising about the body can help health care professionals better tailor their care to individual patients by helping them better understand how illness or disability affect the life of the patient.[13] Likewise, consider a classical phenomenological distinction such as that between the time of the clock and lived time. Consider how the experience of time can change as a result of a diagnosis. Consider how it might affect short- and long-term planning, consider how it might change one's experience of the openness of the future. Consider how an hour in pain, or an hour waiting for treatment, might feel much longer than an hour spent watching an exciting movie, even though the hour still contains the same number of minutes.

The relevance of phenomenology for health care is not restricted to these kinds of analyses, however. Phenomenology also offers insights of a more systemic nature. One interesting example can be found in an older study by Ashworth and colleagues.[14] The idea that patients should be actively involved in rather than simply passive recipients of health care decisions is widespread and has in particular been considered decisive for increased patient compliance. But what is the right way to involve the patient and what are the obstacles to such involvement? In order to address these questions, the authors turned to Schutz and his work on social interaction. They briefly presented some of his core ideas, and in particular highlighted Schutz's discussion of the social distribution of knowledge. The authors then proceeded to show how these ideas might be used in everyday clinical practice. Participation is always contextual; it is participation in a shared cultural practice that often relies on a number of taken-for-granted assumptions. One obvious challenge to proper patient participation is that the patients are encouraged and invited to participate in a medical setting involving specific tasks, procedures, aims, roles, and statuses that they are often quite unfamiliar with, and where they and the health care professionals are not at all on equal footing. Whereas the nurses are trained experts who are thoroughly familiar with all the standards and routines connected to admission, history taking, ward rounds, discharge, etc., many of these procedures will be quite bewildering to the patients, who will attempt to make sense of them on the basis of their own past experiences. The mismatch between the nurses' and patients' stock of knowledge can easily lead to miscommunication and misunderstanding. Indeed, the very attempt by the nurses to actively involve the patients in their own health care decision, might even come as a surprise to the patients and be interpreted as evidence of the nurses' lack of care and concern. If the nurses are to succeed in involving the patients in genuinely patient-centred care, it is consequently crucial that the nurses are aware of and recognise the patients' varied life experiences.

Summing up, using phenomenology in a clinical context is rarely about being concerned with the ultimate subject-dependent nature of reality, nor is it simply a question of showing an unprejudiced interest in the patient's experiential descriptions. Part of the task is precisely to apply a mindset and a theoretical framework that will allow one to capture the fundamental structures of the changed life situation. How is your very being-in-the-world transformed if you are living with schizophrenia, cerebral palsy, or hemispatial neglect? How does illness, disability, or disorder affect your relation to yourself, to the world, and to others?

★

Let me in conclusion outline three challenges that current research and practice is confronted with when it comes to a successful engagement with phenomenology.

The first challenge is that of being *too superficial*. Occasionally, a study is presented as phenomenological simply because it contains careful first-person descriptions of experience. But is it really appropriate to qualify a study or an approach as phenomenological merely because it considers the perspective of the informant, is qualitative and non-reductive, and seeks to provide rich experiential descriptions? Would such an approach really differ from other approaches in qualitative research, would such a study allow for insights that one could not have obtained otherwise? Is there not far more to phenomenology than simply being open-minded and interested in first-person experience?

A possible remedy against the superficiality charge is to engage with the classical texts and seek inspiration from them. Indeed, it seems reasonable to expect any researcher or practitioner who claims to be using a phenomenological method, procedure, or approach to have some familiarity with phenomenological theory. This immediately confronts us with the next challenge, however, which is that of being *too philosophical*, i.e., operating with too many technical philosophical concepts or methodological requirements whose concrete relevance remains unclear. It is essential that phenomenology is being used in a transparent way, i.e., in such a way that it is clear which elements are being used and what role they are supposed to play. A certain pragmatism is consequently appropriate. One should only employ concepts and methodological tools that are pertinent for the task at hand, and which can allow for new insights or better therapeutic interventions. The pursuit of purity and orthodoxy is a red herring.

This finally brings me to the third charge, which is that of remaining *too insular*. Over the years, phenomenology has found use in a variety of disciplines. Somewhat surprisingly, however, insights from one successful disciplinary application have rarely been taken up by other disciplines. Occasionally, the understanding of what is happening in other disciplines is not only limited but quite mistaken. To claim that phenomenological psychiatrists like Jaspers, Minkowski, and Binswanger have offered "multiple insights and revisionist understandings of the conduct of psychotherapy" and that these therapists "did modify their practices but it was done on an individual basis and it was therapeutic practice, not research"[15] as Giorgi has recently done, manages to mischaracterise in a rather fundamental way, what the tradition of phenomenological psychiatry has to offer. This is a missed opportunity. The way forward is to collaborate across the disciplines and to draw on and learn from exemplary approaches and best practice models.

What is then the outcome of these reflections? As should hopefully be apparent, I am not proposing that phenomenology should not be applied. Phenomenology has over the years provided crucial inputs to a whole range of empirical disciplines. The reason it has been able to do this so successfully is partially because phenomenology is far from merely being a descriptive enterprise. Phenomenology also offers theoretical accounts of its own that can challenge existing models and background assumptions.

Ultimately, anybody interested in an empirical use of phenomenology should not primarily look to it as a rigorous method, but as an open-minded attitude and theoretical framework that can be used in conjunction with a variety of methods. Nurses, physiotherapists, psychologists, educators, psychiatrists, anthropologists, etc. who wish to draw on phenomenology should adopt a pragmatic attitude and be less concerned with whether or not the procedure accords with Husserl's, Heidegger's, or Merleau-Ponty's own cursory instructions about how to develop a non-philosophical phenomenology. Of far more importance is whether the phenomenological tools being employed are pertinent, whether they allow for new insights or better therapeutic interventions, i.e., whether they make a valuable difference to the scientific community and/or the clients.

NOTES

1   Spiegelberg, H. (1972). *Phenomenology in Psychology and Psychiatry*. Evanston, IL: Northwestern University Press: 366.
2   Binswanger, L. (1922). *Einführung in die Probleme der Allgemeinen Psychologie*. Berlin: Verlag von Julius Springer: 176, 242.
3   Binswanger, L. (1922). *Einführung in die Probleme der Allgemeinen Psychologie*. Berlin: Verlag von Julius Springer: 233–234.
4   Binswanger, L. (1922). *Einführung in die Probleme der Allgemeinen Psychologie*. Berlin: Verlag von Julius Springer: 242.
5   Giorgi, A. (2010). Phenomenology and the practice of science. *Existential Analysis* 21(1): 18.
6   Morley, J. (2010). It's always about the epoché. *Les Collectifs du Cirp* 1: 223–232.
7   Husserl, E. (1970). *The Crisis of European Sciences and Transcendental Phenomenology: An Introduction to Phenomenological Philosophy*, trans. D. Carr. Evanston, IL: Northwestern University Press: 180.
8   Giorgi, A. (2012). The descriptive phenomenological psychological method. *Journal of Phenomenological Psychology* 43(1): 4.
9   Langdridge, D. 2008. Phenomenology and critical social psychology: Directions and debates in theory of research. *Social and Personality Psychology Compass* 2(3): 1129.

10 Paley, J. (2013). 5 questions. In A. Forss, C. Ceci, and J.S. Drummond (eds.), *Philosophy of Nursing: 5 Questions* (pp. 143–155). Copenhagen: Automatic Press: 148.

11 Burch, M. (2021). Make applied phenomenology what it needs to be: An interdisciplinary research program. *Continental Philosophy Review* 54: 276.

12 Carel, H. (2013). Bodily doubt. *Journal of Consciousness Studies* 20(7–8): 184.

13 See, for example: Leder, D. (1990). *The Absent Body*. Chicago, IL: University of Chicago Press; Toombs, S.K. (1992). *The Meaning of Illness: A Phenomenological Account of the Different Perspectives of Physician and Patient*. Dordrecht: Kluwer; Svenaeus, F. (2000). *The Hermeneutics of Medicine and the Phenomenology of Health: Steps Towards a Philosophy of Medical Practice*. Dordrecht: Kluwer.

14 Ashworth, P.D., Longmate, M.A., and Morrison, P. (1992). Patient participation: Its meaning and significance in the context of caring. *Journal of Advanced Nursing* 17: 1430–1439.

15 Giorgi, A. (2020). In defence of scientific phenomenologies. *Journal of Phenomenological Psychology* 51: 154–155.

SUGGESTIONS FOR FURTHER READING

Havi Carel, *Phenomenology of Illness*. Oxford: Oxford University Press, 2016.

Anthony Fernandez and Steven Crowell (eds.), *The Phenomenological Method Today*. Special issue of *Continental Philosophy Review* 54, 2021, 119–293.

CONCLUSION

Steven Crowell once remarked that the future prospects of phenomenology will depend on the talent of those who take it up.[1] I think this is quite correct – and that it holds true in the case of both philosophical phenomenology and applied phenomenology. I also think, however, that it will depend upon the ability to articulate and strengthen what is common to the phenomenological enterprise instead of getting involved in the kind of sectarian trench warfare that has regrettably plagued the history of phenomenology at various points of time. Too much energy has been devoted to highlighting internal differences, rather than common strengths.

For a while, phenomenology was out of fashion, replaced and superseded by other theory formations such as critical theory, structuralism, and deconstruction. There is no question, however, that phenomenology has had something of a revival during the last 20–30 years. There are many reasons for this, but one of them is that the facile dismissal of the subject of experience in favour of a focus on sign systems, language games, discourses, etc. has been found wanting. Contrary to a widespread misunderstanding, the central claim of phenomenology has never been that an investigation of subjectivity is sufficient if we want to understand the natural, historical, social, and cultural realm. The claim was rather that such an investigation is

DOI: 10.4324/9781003350682-17

necessary and indispensable. If we want to understand the world we are living in, we need to factor in the role played by embodied, perceiving, thinking, and feeling agents, and here phenomenology has something important to offer.

Far from being simply a tradition of the past, phenomenology is quite alive and in a position to make valuable contributions to contemporary thought. As the contributions collected in *The Oxford Handbook of Contemporary Phenomenology* show,[2] a lot of work is currently being done in two directions: Inward (and backward) and outward (and forward). On the one hand, we find a continuing engagement and conversation with the classical authors. The philosophical resources and insights to be found in the work of Husserl, Scheler, Stein, Walther, Heidegger, Sartre, Beauvoir, Merleau-Ponty, Levinas, etc., are evidently not yet exhausted. On the other hand, an increasing amount of dialogue is taking place between phenomenology and other philosophical traditions and empirical disciplines. In my view, phenomenology should continue to pursue this two-pronged strategy. It is hard to predict how many self-avowed phenomenologists there will be 100 years from now. But I am quite confident that the basic insights found in phenomenology will continue to appeal to and attract and inspire gifted thinkers.

NOTES

1 Crowell, S. (2002). Is there a phenomenological research program? *Synthese* 131(3): 442.
2 Zahavi, D. (ed.) (2012). *The Oxford Handbook of Contemporary Phenomenology*. Oxford: Oxford University Press.

SUGGESTIONS FOR FURTHER READING

Dan Zahavi (ed.), *The Oxford Handbook of Contemporary Phenomenology*. Oxford: Oxford University Press, 2012.

GLOSSARY

Alterity Being other or different. The term is often used to refer to the otherness of a foreign subject.

Being-in-the-world (*In-der-Welt-sein*) A composite term introduced by Heidegger to designate the world-embedded character of the mind and the extent to which mind and world are intertwined and co-dependent.

Being-with (*Mitsein*) A Heideggerian term meant to capture the idea that our relationship with others is a fundamental and defining feature of our intentional being.

Cogitatum The object of thought, or, more generally, the intentional object.

Cogito The act of thinking, or, more generally, the intentional act.

Computationalism The view that mental states are computational states, and that the mind works as an information-processing machine.

Constitution The subjective process through which something (typically an object) is revealed, disclosed, or brought to manifestation.

Correlation The dependency relations between act and object, mind and world.

Dasein Heidegger's term for the intentional subject. The term is composed of "Da", meaning "there", and "sein", meaning "being", i.e., there-being or being-there, and emphasises the extent to which our very being is to be located in and involved with the world.

Eidetic variation An imaginatively guided analysis that seeks to disclose the essential features of the topic under investigation.

Empathy The experiential encounter with another subject's embodied and embedded experience.

Epistemology Theory of knowledge.

Epoché The suspension or bracketing of a certain dogmatic (natural) attitude vis-à-vis the world, e.g., our belief in the mind-independent existence of the world.

Essentialism The idea that an entity has a certain set of invariant features that are essential to its identity, which makes it what it is, and which it cannot lack without ceasing to be that kind of entity.

Facticity The contingency of human existence, nature, history; that which cannot be deduced or justified by pure reasoning.

Historicity The fundamental historical character of human existence; the fact that human understanding isn't merely temporal, but also situated in a historical context and tradition.

Horizon The background or context within which any object of experience is situated. It provides the sense that there is always more to be discovered or understood about any object than that which is actually given.

Idealism The term has many different meanings and definitions, and is here primarily used to refer to the view that reality is in some sense mind-dependent.

Idiographic approach A focus on individual cases and particular events (rather than on essential features or universal laws).

Intentionality The idea that consciousness is characterised by being of, or about, or directed at something.

Intersubjectivity The relation between subjects.

Körper The physical and biological body; the body considered as a physical object that belongs to nature.

Leib The lived and experienced body; the body as subjectively lived through.

Lifeworld The world we live in, the pre-theoretical world of experience we take for granted in daily life.

Metaphysics A term with many meanings. Here, primarily used to designate a concern with whether or not reality is mind-independent.

Mitwelt A notion used by Schutz to designate the world of our contemporaries, i.e., those that exist simultaneously with us, but who are not bodily present in our immediate vicinity.

Natural attitude The pervasive pre-philosophical assumption that the world can be taken for granted and exists independently of us.

Naturalism The idea that everything that exists can be studied by the methods of natural science and be reduced to natural-scientific facts.

Neurophenomenology The proposal that one should incorporate phenomenological forms of investigation into the experimental protocols of neuroscientific research on consciousness.

Objectivism The view that reality is what it is completely independently of any experiencer, and that our cognitive apprehension of reality is at best a faithful mirroring of a mind-independent world.

Ontology The study of the fundamental features of reality.

Phenomenology, generative A study of the constitutive role of transgenerational, historical, and sociocultural factors, e.g., how the constitutive accomplishments of previous generations affect our individual experiences.

Phenomenology, genetic A study of the correlation between act and object that examines the temporal becoming of different forms of intentionality.

Phenomenology, static A study of the correlation between act and object that disregards origin and development.

Pictorial intentionality Our awareness of pictures and of what they depict.

Present–at–hand That which we encounter when we adopt a theoretical or spectatorial attitude.

Proprioception The position sense that I have with respect to my limbs and overall posture. It is the sense that allows me to know whether my legs are crossed, or not, without looking at them.

Ready–to–hand That which is available to us in our practical concerns and engagement, prior to any theorising or detached observation.

Reduction, eidetic The laying bare of the essential features of the topic under consideration.

Reduction, transcendental The systematic analysis of the constitutive function of consciousness, of how mind and world are constitutively interrelated.

Reductionism The idea that we can and should explain a certain phenomenon or property in terms of simpler and more basic properties.

Representationalism The view that our cognitive access to reality is in some way mediated by representations.

Scientism The view that the methods of natural science provide the sole means of epistemic access to the world, and that entities that cannot be captured in terms accepted by natural science are non-existent.

Sedimentation The way in which that which is acquired in experience settles down, becomes habitualised, and informs, enables, and constrains future experiences.

Sociology of knowledge The study of the societal conditions for the formation, maintenance, and distribution or stratification of diverse types of knowledge.

Theory of mind The idea that our understanding of the psychological life of others is inferential in nature and enabled by some kind of (psychological) theory.

Transcendental philosophy A systematic concern with the (subjective) conditions of possibility for objectivity.

Typification the process by which individuals make sense of the social world by classifying or grouping people, objects, or processes into specific categories.

Umwelt The world of our immediate surroundings.

REFERENCES

Ahmed, S. (2007). A phenomenology of whiteness. *Feminist Theory* 8(2): 149–168.

Anderson, E. (2010). *The Imperative of Integration*. Princeton, NJ: Princeton University Press.

Ashworth, P.D., Longmate, M.A., and Morrison, P. (1992). Patient participation: Its meaning and significance in the context of caring. *Journal of Advanced Nursing* 17: 1430–1439.

Beauvoir, S. de (1953). *The Second Sex*, trans. H.M. Parshley. London: Jonathan Cape.

Beauvoir, S. de (1965). *The Prime of Life*, trans. P. Green. Harmondsworth: Penguin Books.

Beauvoir, S. de (2018). *The Ethics of Ambiguity*, trans. B. Frechtman. New York, NY: Open Road Media.

Beck, T.J. (2013). A phenomenological analysis of anxiety as experienced in social situations. *Journal of Phenomenological Psychology* 44(2): 179–219.

Berger, P.L. and Luckmann, T. (1991). *The Social Construction of Reality: A Treatise in the Sociology of Knowledge*. Harmondsworth: Penguin Books.

Binswanger, L. (1922). *Einführung in die Probleme der Allgemeinen Psychologie*. Berlin: Verlag von Julius Springer.

Borrett, D., Kelly, S., and Kwan, H. (2000). Bridging embodied cognition and brain function: The role of phenomenology. *Philosophical Psychology* 13(2): 261–266.

Bortolan, A. and Magrì, E. (eds.) (2022). *Empathy, Intersubjectivity, and the Social World*. Berlin: De Gruyter.

Burch, M. (2021). Make applied phenomenology what it needs to be: An interdisciplinary research program. *Continental Philosophy Review* 54: 275–293.

Caputo, J.D. (1977). The question of being and transcendental phenomenology: Reflections on Heidegger's relationship to Husserl. *Research in Phenomenology* 7(1): 84–105.

Carel, H. (2013). Bodily doubt. *Journal of Consciousness Studies* 20(7–8): 178–197.

Carel, H. (2016). *Phenomenology of Illness*. Oxford: Oxford University Press.

Carman, T. (2003). *Heidegger's Analytic: Interpretation, Discourse and Authenticity in Being and Time*. Cambridge: Cambridge University Press.

Churchill, S.D. and Wertz, F.J. (2015). An introduction to phenomenological research in psychology: Historical, conceptual, and methodological foundations. In K.J. Schneider and J.F. Pierson (eds.), *The Handbook of Humanistic Psychology: Leading Edges in Theory, Research, and Practice* (pp. 275–295). Thousand Oaks, CA: Sage.

Churchland, P.M. (1988). *Matter and Consciousness: A Contemporary Introduction to the Philosophy of Mind*. Revised edn. Cambridge, MA: MIT Press.

Cole, J.D. (1995). *Pride and a Daily Marathon*. Cambridge, MA: MIT Press.

Crowell, S. (2002). Is there a phenomenological research program? *Synthese* 131(3): 419–444.

Crowell, S. (2005). Heidegger and Husserl: The matter and method of philosophy. In H.L. Dreyfus and M.A. Wrathall (eds.), *A Companion to Heidegger* (pp. 49–64). Oxford: Blackwell.

Dastur, F. (2024). French phenomenology after 1961. In M. Sinclair and D. Whistler (eds.), *The Oxford Handbook of Modern French Philosophy* (pp. 319–333). Oxford: Oxford University Press.

Derrida, J. (1995). Violence and metaphysics: An essay on the thought of Emmanuel Levinas. In J. Derrida, *Writing and Difference*, trans. Alan Bass (pp. 79–153). London: Routledge.

Dillon, M.C. (1983). Merleau-Ponty and the reversibility thesis. *Man and World* 16(4): 365–388.

Dillon, M.C. (1988). *Merleau-Ponty's Ontology*. 2nd edn. Evanston, IL: Northwestern University Press.

Dolezal, L. (2015). *The Body and Shame: Phenomenology, Feminism, and the Socially Shaped Body*. Lanham, MD: Lexington Books.

Dorfman, E. (2009). History of the lifeworld: From Husserl to Merleau-Ponty. *Philosophy Today* 53(3): 294–303.

Doyon, M. (2024). *Phenomenology and the Norms of Perception*. Oxford: Oxford University Press.

Drummond, J.D. (2012). Intentionality without representationalism. In D. Zahavi (ed.), *The Oxford Handbook of Contemporary Phenomenology* (pp. 115–133). Oxford: Oxford University Press.

Fanon, F. (2008). *Black Skin, White Masks*, trans. C.L. Markmann. London: Pluto Press.

Fernandez, A. and Crowell, S. (eds.) (2021). *The Phenomenological Method Today*. Special issue of *Continental Philosophy Review* 54: 119–293.

Finlay, L. (2009). Debating phenomenological research methods. *Phenomenology & Practice* 3(1): 6–25.

Fodor, J. (1987). *Psychosemantics*. Cambridge, MA: MIT Press.

From, F. (1953). *Om Oplevelsen af Andres Adfærd: Et Bidrag til den Menneskelige Adfærds Fænomenologi*. København: Nyt Nordisk Forlag.

Galileo, G. (1957). *Discoveries and Opinions of Galileo*. New York, NY: Anchor House.

Gallagher, S. (1997). Mutual enlightenment: Recent phenomenology in cognitive science. *Journal of Consciousness Studies* 4(3): 195–214.

Gallagher, S. (2003). Phenomenology and experimental design: Toward a phenomenologically enlightened experimental science. *Journal of Consciousness Studies* 10(9–10): 85–99.

Gallagher, S. (2007). Simulation trouble. *Social Neuroscience* 2(3–4): 353–365.

Gallagher, S. and Cole, J. (1995). Body image and body schema in a deafferented subject. *Journal of Mind and Behavior* 16(4): 369–390.

Gallagher, S. and Meltzoff, A.N. (1996). The earliest sense of self and others: Merleau-Ponty and recent developmental studies. *Philosophical Psychology* 9(2): 211–233.

Gallagher, S. and Zahavi, D. (2021). *The Phenomenological Mind*. 3rd edn. London: Routledge.

Giorgi, A. (1994). A phenomenological perspective on certain qualitative research methods. *Journal of Phenomenological Psychology* 25(2): 190–220.

Giorgi, A. (2009). *The Descriptive Phenomenological Method in Psychology: A Modified Husserlian Approach*. Pittsburgh, PA: Duquesne University Press.

Giorgi, A. (2010). Phenomenology and the practice of science. *Existential Analysis* 21(1): 3–22.

Giorgi, A. (2012). The descriptive phenomenological psychological method. *Journal of Phenomenological Psychology* 43(1): 3–12.

Giorgi, A. (2017). Review essay: A response to the attempted critique of the scientific phenomenological method. *Journal of Phenomenological Psychology* 48(1): 83–144.

Giorgi, A. (2020). In defence of scientific phenomenologies. *Journal of Phenomenological Psychology* 51: 135–161.

Guenther, L. (2013). *Solitary Confinement*. Minneapolis, MN: University of Minnesota Press.

Guenther, L. (2020). Critical phenomenology. In G. Weiss, A.V. Murphy, and G. Salamon (eds.), *50 Concepts for a Critical Phenomenology* (pp. 11–16). Evanston, IL: Northwestern University Press.

Guenther, L. (2021). Six senses of critique for critical phenomenology. *Puncta: Journal of Critical Phenomenology* 4(2): 5–23.

Gurwitsch, A. (1979). *Human Encounters in the Social World.* Pittsburgh, PA: Duquesne University Press.

Habermas, J. (1992). *Postmetaphysical Thinking*, trans. W.M. Hohengarten. Cambridge, MA: MIT Press.

Hanna, R. (2014). Husserl's crisis and our crisis. *International Journal of Philosophical Studies* 22(5): 752–770.

Hansen, C.R. and Karpatschof, B. (eds.) (2001). *Københavnerfænomenologien, Bisat eller Genfødt?* København: Danmarks Pædagogiske Universitet.

Hart, J. (1992). *The Person and the Common Life: Studies in a Husserlian Social Ethics.* Dordrecht: Kluwer Academic Publishers.

Heidegger, M. (1982). *The Basic Problems of Phenomenology*, trans. A. Hofstadter. Bloomington, IN: Indiana University Press.

Heidegger, M. (1985). *History of the Concept of Time: Prolegomena*, trans. T. Kisiel. Bloomington, IN: Indiana University Press.

Heidegger, M. (1993a). *Basic Writings*, ed. by D.F. Krell. San Francisco, CA: Harper.

Heidegger, M. (1993b). *Grundprobleme der Phänomenologie (1919/1920)*. Gesamtausgabe Band 58. Frankfurt am Main: Vittorio Klostermann.

Heidegger, M. (1996). *Being and Time*, trans. J. Stambaugh. Albany, NY: SUNY.

Heidegger, M. (1998). *Pathmarks*, ed. by W. McNeill. Cambridge: Cambridge University Press.

Heidegger, M. (2001). *Einleitung in die Philosophie.* Gesamtausgabe Band 27. Frankfurt am Main: Vittorio Klostermann.

Heidegger, M. (2003). *Four Seminars*, trans. A. Mitchell and F. Raffoul. Bloomington, IN: Indiana University Press.

Heidegger, M. (2009). *Logic as the Question Concerning the Essence of Language*, trans. W.T. Gregory and Y. Unna. Albany, NY: SUNY.

Heidegger, M. (2010). *Logic: The Question of Truth*, trans. T. Sheehan. Bloomington, IN: Indiana University Press.

Heimann, K., Høffding, S., and Martiny, K. (eds.) (2023). *Phenomenological Interviews: Working with Others' Experiences.* Special Issue of *Phenomenology and the Cognitive Sciences* 22: 1–311.

Heinämaa, S. (2003). *Toward a Phenomenology of Sexual Difference: Husserl, Merleau-Ponty, Beauvoir.* Lanham, MD: Rowman & Littlefield.

Heinämaa, S., Hartimo, M., and Miettinen, T. (eds.) (2014). *Phenomenology and the Transcendental.* London: Routledge.

Held, K. (2003). Husserl's phenomenology of the life-world. In D. Welton (ed.), *The New Husserl: A Critical Reader* (pp. 32–62). Bloomington, IN: Indiana University Press.

Henriksen, M.G., Parnas, J., and Zahavi, D. (2019). Thought insertion and disturbed for-me-ness (minimal selfhood) in schizophrenia. *Consciousness and Cognition* 74: 102770.

Henry, M. (1973). *The Essence of Manifestation*, trans. G. Etzkorn. The Hague: Martinus Nijhoff.

Herrmann, S., Thonhauser, G., Loidolt, S., Matzner, T., and Baratella, N. (eds.) (2024). *The Routledge Handbook of Political Phenomenology*. London: Routledge.

Høffding, S. and Martiny, K. (2016). Framing a phenomenological interview: What, why and how. *Phenomenology and the Cognitive Sciences* 15(4): 539–564.

Hopp, W. (2020). *Phenomenology: A Contemporary Introduction*. London: Routledge.

Husserl, E. (1959). *Erste Philosophie (1923/24). Zweiter Teil. Theorie der Phänomenologischen Reduktion*, ed. by R. Boehm. Husserliana 8. The Hague: Martinus Nijhoff.

Husserl, E. (1960). *Cartesian Meditations: An Introduction to Phenomenology*, trans. D. Cairns. The Hague: Martinus Nijhoff.

Husserl, E. (1962). *Phänomenologische Psychologie. Vorlesungen Sommersemester 1925*, ed. by W. Biemel. Husserliana 9. The Hague: Martinus Nijhoff.

Husserl, E. (1965). Philosophy as rigorous science. In Q. Lauer (trans.), *Phenomenology and the Crisis of Philosophy* (pp. 71–147). New York, NY: Harper & Row.

Husserl, E. (1969). *Formal and Transcendental Logic*, trans. D. Cairns. The Hague: Martinus Nijhoff.

Husserl, E. (1970). *The Crisis of European Sciences and Transcendental Phenomenology: An Introduction to Phenomenological Philosophy*, trans. D. Carr. Evanston, IL: Northwestern University Press.

Husserl, E. (1973a). *Zur Phänomenologie der Intersubjektivität II. Texte aus dem Nachlass. Zweiter Teil. 1921–1928*, ed. by I. Kern. Husserliana 14. The Hague: Martinus Nijhoff.

Husserl, E. (1973b). *Zur Phänomenologie der Intersubjektivität III. Texte aus dem Nachlass. Dritter Teil. 1929–1935*, ed. by I. Kern. Husserliana 15. The Hague: Martinus Nijhoff.

Husserl, E. (1977). *Phenomenological Psychology: Lectures, Summer Semester, 1925*, trans. J. Scanlon. The Hague: Martinus Nijhoff.

Husserl, E. (1981). *Shorter Works*, ed. by P. McCormick and F.A. Elliston. Notre Dame, IN: University of Notre Dame Press.

Husserl, E. (1982). *Ideas Pertaining to a Pure Phenomenology and to a Phenomenological Philosophy. First Book. General Introduction to a Pure Phenomenology*, trans. F. Kersten. The Hague: Martinus Nijhoff.

Husserl, E. (1989). *Ideas Pertaining to a Pure Phenomenology and to a Phenomenological Philosophy. Second Book. Studies in the Phenomenology of Constitution*, trans. R. Rojcewicz and A. Schuwer. Dordrecht: Kluwer Academic Publishers.

Husserl, E. (1997). *Psychological and Transcendental Phenomenology and the Confrontation with Heidegger (1927–1931)*, ed. and trans. T. Sheehan and R.E. Palmer. Dordrecht: Kluwer Academic Publishers.

Husserl, E. (2001a). *Die "Bernauer Manuskripte" über das Zeitbewußtsein (1917/18)*, ed. by R. Bernet and D. Lohmar. Husserliana 33. Dordrecht: Kluwer Academic Publishers.

Husserl, E. (2001b). *Logical Investigations I–II*, trans. J.N. Findlay. London: Routledge.

Husserl, E. (2001c). *Analyses Concerning Passive and Active Synthesis: Lectures on Transcendental Logic*, trans. A. Steinbock. Dordrecht: Kluwer Academic Publishers.

Husserl, E. (2002). *Zur phänomenologischen Reduktion: Texte aus dem Nachlass (1926–1935)*, ed. by S. Luft. Husserliana 34. Dordrecht: Kluwer Academic Publishers.

Husserl, E. (2005). *Phantasy, Image Consciousness, and Memory (1898–1925)*, trans. J.B. Brough. Dordrecht: Springer.

Jacobs, H. (ed.) (2021). *The Husserlian Mind*. London: Routledge.

Jansen, J. (2022). Phenomenology and critique: On "mere" description and its normative dimensions. In A.S. Aldea, D. Carr, and S. Heinämaa (eds.), *Phenomenology as Critique: Why Method Matters* (pp. 44–55). London: Routledge.

Jaspers, K. (1912). Die phänomenologische forschungsrichtung in der psychopathologie. *Zeitschrift für die gesamte Neurologie und Psychiatrie* 9: 391–408.

Jaspers, K. (1963). *General Psychopathology*, trans. J. Hoenig and M.W. Hamilton. Manchester: Manchester University Press.

Katz, D. (1989). *The World of Touch*, trans. L.E. Krueger. Hillsdale, NJ: Lawrence Erlbaum Associates.

Katz, D. (1999). *The World of Colour*, trans. R.B. MacLeod and C.W. Fox. Abingdon: Routledge.

Kockelmans, J.J. (ed.) (1987). *Phenomenological Psychology: The Dutch School*. Dordrecht: Springer.

Køster, A. and Fernandez, A.V. (2023). Investigating modes of being in the world: An introduction to phenomenologically grounded qualitative research. *Phenomenology and the Cognitive Sciences* 22(1): 149–169.

Laing, R.D. (1963). Minkowski and schizophrenia. *Review of Existential Psychology and Psychiatry* 3(3): 195–207.

Langdridge, D. 2008. Phenomenology and critical social psychology: Directions and debates in theory of research. *Social and Personality Psychology Compass* 2(3): 1126–1142.

Leder, D. (1990). *The Absent Body*. Chicago, IL: University of Chicago Press.

Lenkowski, W.J. (1978). What is Husserl's epoche? The problem of beginning of philosophy in a Husserlian context. *Man and World* 11(3–4): 299–323.

Levinas, E. (1969). *Totality and Infinity: An Essay on Exteriority*, trans. A. Lingis. Pittsburgh, PA: Duquesne University Press.

Levinas, E. (1987). *Time and the Other*, trans. R.A. Cohen. Pittsburgh, PA: Duquesne University Press.

Levinas, E. (1998). *Discovering Existence with Husserl*, trans. R.A. Cohen and M.B. Smith. Evanston, IL: Northwestern University Press.

Lincoln, Y.S. and Guba, E.G. (2013). *The Constructivist Credo*. Walnut Creek, CA: Left Coast Press.

Linschoten, J. (1987). On falling asleep. In J.J. Kockelmans (ed.), *Phenomenological Psychology: The Dutch School* (pp. 79–117). Dordrecht: Springer.

Loidolt, S. (2024). Plural beginnings, ambivalent heritage. In S. Herrmann, G. Thonhauser, S. Loidolt, T. Matzner, and N. Baratella (eds.), *The Routledge Handbook of Political Phenomenology* (pp. 11–17). London: Routledge.

Lutz, A. and Thompson, E. (2003). Neurophenomenology: Integrating subjective experience and brain dynamics in the neuroscience of consciousness. *Journal of Consciousness Studies* 10(9–10): 31–52.

Lutz, A., Lachaux, J.-P., Martinerie, J., and Varela, F.J. (2002). Guiding the study of brain dynamics by using first-person data: Synchrony patterns correlate with ongoing conscious states during a simple visual task. *Proceedings of the National Academy of Sciences* 99(3): 1586–1591.

MacLeod, R.B. (1954). David Katz 1884–1953. *Psychological Review* 61(1): 1–4.

Madison, G.B. (1981). *The Phenomenology of Merleau-Ponty*. Athens, OH: Ohio University.

Magrì, E. and McQueen, P. (2023). *Critical Phenomenology: An Introduction*. Cambridge: Polity Press.

Meindl, P. and Zahavi, D. (2023). From communication to communalization: A Husserlian account. *Continental Philosophy Review* 56(3): 361–377.

Merleau-Ponty, M. (1963). *The Structure of Behavior*, trans. A.L. Fisher. Boston, MA: Beacon Press.

Merleau-Ponty, M. (1964a). *Signs*, trans. R.C. McClearly. Evanston, IL: Northwestern University Press.

Merleau-Ponty, M. (1964b). *Sense and Non-Sense*, trans. H. Dreyfus and P. Dreyfus. Evanston, IL: Northwestern University Press.

Merleau-Ponty, M. (1964c). *The Primacy of Perception*, ed. by J.M. Edie. Evanston, IL: Northwestern University Press.

Merleau-Ponty, M. (2012). *Phenomenology of Perception,* trans. D.A. Landes. London: Routledge.

Minkowski, E. (2019). *Lived Time: Phenomenological and Psychopathological Studies*, trans. N. Metzel. Evanston, IL: Northwestern University Press.

Møller, P., Haug, E., Raballo, A., Parnas, J., and Melle, I. (2011). Examination of anomalous self-experience in first-episode psychosis: Interrater reliability. *Psychopathology* 44(6): 386–390.

Moran, D. (2000). *Introduction to Phenomenology*. London: Routledge.

Morley, J. (2010). It's always about the epoché. *Les Collectifs du Cirp* 1: 223–232.

Nelson, B., Thompson, A., and Yung, A.R. (2013). Not all first-episode psychosis is the same: Preliminary evidence of greater basic self-disturbance in schizophrenia spectrum cases. *Early Intervention in Psychiatry* 7(2): 200–204.

Oksala, J. (2023). The method of critical phenomenology: Simone de Beauvoir as a phenomenologist. *European Journal of Philosophy* 31(1): 137–150.

Paley, J. (1997). Husserl, phenomenology and nursing. *Journal of Advanced Nursing* 26(1): 187–193.

Paley, J. (2005). Phenomenology as rhetoric. *Nursing Inquiry* 12(2): 106–116.

Paley, J. (2013). 5 questions. In A. Forss, C. Ceci, and J.S. Drummond (eds.), *Philosophy of Nursing: 5 Questions* (pp. 143–155). Copenhagen: Automatic Press.

Paley, J. (2017). *Phenomenology as Qualitative Research: A Critical Analysis of Meaning Attribution*. London: Routledge.

Parnas, J., Møller, P., Kircher, T., Thalbitzer, J., Jansson, L., Handest, P., and Zahavi, D. (2005). EASE: Examination of anomalous self-experience. *Psychopathology* 38(5): 236–258.

Petitot, J., Varela, F.J., Pachoud, B., and Roy, J.-M. (eds.) (1999). *Naturalizing Phenomenology*. Stanford, CA: Stanford University Press.

Petrovskaya, O. (2014), Nursing phenomenology after Paley. *Nursing Philosophy* 15: 60–71.

Rochat, P. and Striano, T. (1999). Social-cognitive development in the first year. In P. Rochat (ed.), *Early Social Cognition: Understanding Others in the First Months of Life* (pp. 3–34). Hillsdale, NJ: Lawrence Erlbaum Associates.

Rodemeyer, L.M. (2022). A phenomenological critique of critical phenomenology. In A.S. Aldea, D. Carr, and S. Heinämaa (eds.), *Phenomenology as Critique: Why Method Matters* (pp. 95–112). London: Routledge.

Romdenh-Romluc, K. (2010). *Merleau-Ponty and Phenomenology of Perception*. London: Routledge.

Roy, J.-M., Petitot, J., Pachoud, B., and Varela, F.J. (1999). Beyond the gap: An introduction to naturalizing phenomenology. In J. Petitot, F.J. Varela, B. Pachoud, and J.-M. Roy (eds.), *Naturalizing Phenomenology* (pp. 1–83). Stanford, CA: Stanford University Press.

Salamon, G. (2018). What is critical about critical phenomenology? *Puncta: Journal of Critical Phenomenology* 1: 8–17.

Sartre, J.-P. (1970). Intentionality: A fundamental idea of Husserl's phenomenology. *Journal of the British Society for Phenomenology* 1(2): 4–5.

Sartre, J.-P. (1995). *Anti-Semite and Jew*, trans. G.J. Becker. New York, NY: Shocken Books.

Sartre, J.-P. (2003). *Being and Nothingness*, trans. H.E. Barnes. London: Routledge.

Sass, L.A. and Parnas, J. (2003). Schizophrenia, consciousness, and the self. *Schizophrenia Bulletin* 29(3): 427–444.

Scheler, M. (1973). *Formalism in Ethics and Non-Formal Ethics of Values: A New Attempt Toward a Foundation of an Ethical Personalism*, trans. M.S. Frings and R.L. Funk. Evanston, IL: Northwestern University Press.

Scheler, M. (2008). *The Nature of Sympathy*, trans. P. Heath. London: Transaction.

Schmid, H.B. (2009). *Plural Action. Essays in Philosophy and Social Science*. Dordrecht: Springer.

Schutz, A. (1962). *The Problem of Social Reality: Collected Papers I*. The Hague: Martinus Nijhoff.

Schutz, A. (1964). *Studies in Social Theory: Collected Papers II*. The Hague: Martinus Nijhoff.

Schutz, A. (1967). *The Phenomenology of the Social World*, trans. G. Walsh and F. Lehnert. Evanston, IL: Northwestern University Press.

Smith, J.A. (1996). Beyond the divide between cognition and discourse: Using interpretative phenomenological analysis in health psychology. *Psychology & Health* 11(2): 261–271.

Smith, J.A. (2018). "Yes it is phenomenological": A reply to Max van Manen's critique of interpretative phenomenological analysis. *Qualitative Health Research* 28: 1955–1958.

Smith, J.A., Flowers, P., and Larkin, M. (2009). *Interpretative Phenomenological Analysis: Theory, Method and Research*. London: Sage.

Smith, J.A. and Osborn, M. (2008). Interpretative phenomenological analysis. In J.A. Smith (ed.), *Qualitative Psychology: A Practical Guide to Research Methods* (pp. 53–80). London: Sage.

Sokolowski, R. (1999). *Introduction to Phenomenology*. Cambridge: Cambridge University Press.

Spiegelberg, H. (1965). *The Phenomenological Movement*. The Hague: Martinus Nijhoff.

Spiegelberg, H. (1972). *Phenomenology in Psychology and Psychiatry*. Evanston, IL: Northwestern University Press.

Stanghellini, G., Broome, M., Fernandez, A. V., Fusar-Poli, P., Raballo, A., and Rosfort, R. (eds.) (2019). *The Oxford Handbook of Phenomenological Psychopathology*. Oxford: Oxford University Press.

Steegmuller, F. (1949). *Maupassant: A Lion in the Path*. London: Macmillan.

Stein, E. (1989). *On the Problem of Empathy*, trans. W. Stein. Washington, DC: ICS Publications.

Steinbock, A.J. (1995). *Home and Beyond: Generative Phenomenology after Husserl.* Evanston, IL: Northwestern University Press.

Stern, D. (2004). *The Present Moment in Psychotherapy and Everyday Life.* New York, NY: W.W. Norton & Company.

Strasser, S. (1963). *Phenomenology and the Human Sciences: A Contribution to a New Scientific Ideal.* Pittsburgh, PA: Duquesne University Press.

Straus, E. (1963). *The Primary World of Senses: A Vindication of Sensory Experience*, trans. J. Needleman. New York, NY: The Free Press of Glencoe.

Svenaeus, F. (2000). *The Hermeneutics of Medicine and the Phenomenology of Health: Steps Towards a Philosophy of Medical Practice.* Dordrecht: Kluwer.

Taipale, J. (2014). *Phenomenology and Embodiment: Husserl and the Constitution of Subjectivity.* Evanston, IL: Northwestern University Press.

Theunissen, M. (1986). *The Other: Studies in the Social Ontology of Husserl, Heidegger, Sartre and Buber*, trans. C. Macann. Cambridge, MA: MIT Press.

Thompson, E. (2007). *Mind in Life: Biology, Phenomenology, and the Sciences of Mind.* Cambridge, MA: Harvard University Press.

Toadvine, T. (2023). Maurice Merleau-Ponty. In E.N. Zalta and U. Nodelman (eds.), *The Stanford Encyclopedia of Philosophy*: https://plato.stanford.edu/archives/win2023/entries/merleau-ponty/.

Toombs, S.K. (1992). *The Meaning of Illness: A Phenomenological Account of the Different Perspectives of Physician and Patient.* Dordrecht: Kluwer.

Trevarthen, C. (1979). Communication and cooperation in early infancy: A description of primary intersubjectivity. In M.M. Bullowa (ed.), *Before Speech: The Beginning of Interpersonal Communication* (pp. 321–347). New York, NY: Cambridge University Press.

van Manen, M. (1990). *Researching Lived Experience: Human Science for an Action Sensitive Pedagogy.* London and Ontario: Althouse Press.

van Manen, M. (2014). *Phenomenology of Practice: Meaning-giving Methods in Phenomenological Research and Writing.* Walnut Creek, CA: Left Coast Press.

van Manen, M. (2017a). But is it phenomenology? *Qualitative Health Research* 27: 775–779.

van Manen, M. (2017b). Phenomenology it its original sense. *Qualitative Health Research* 27: 810–825.

van Manen, M. (2017c). Phenomenology and meaning attribution. *Indo-Pacific Journal of Phenomenology* 17(1): 1–12.

van Manen, M. (2018). Rebuttal rejoinder: Present IPA for what it is— Interpretative psychological analysis. *Qualitative Health Research* 28: 1959–1968.

Varela, F.J. (1996). Neurophenomenology: A methodological remedy for the hard problem. *Journal of Consciousness Studies* 3(4): 330–349.

Varela, F.J. (1997). The naturalization of phenomenology as the transcendence of nature: Searching for generative mutual constraints. *Alter: Revue de Phénoménologie* 5: 355–381.

Varela, F.J., Thompson, E., and Rosch, E. (1991). *The Embodied Mind: Cognitive Science and Human Experience*. Cambridge, MA: MIT Press.

Walther, G. (1923). Zur Ontologie der sozialen Gemeinschaften. In E. Husserl (ed.), *Jahrbuch für Philosophie und Phänomenologische Forschung*, Vol. VI (pp. 1–158). Halle: Max Niemeyer.

Watson, R. (2017). Phenomenology as qualitative research: A critical analysis of meaning attribution John Paley (2016), Routledge, ISBN-13: 978-1138652811. *Nursing Philosophy* 18(4): e12180.

Weiss, G. (1999) *Body Images: Embodiment as Intercorporeality*. London and New York, NY: Routledge.

Weiss, G., Murphy A. V., and Salamon, G. (2020). *50 Concepts for a Critical Phenomenology*. Evanston, IL: Northwestern University Press.

Wood, F.G. (1991). The meaning of caregiving. *Rehabilitation Nursing* 16(4), 195–198.

Young, I.M. (1980). Throwing like a girl: A phenomenology of feminine body comportment, motility and spatiality. *Human Studies* 3: 137–156.

Zahavi, D. (1999a). *Self-awareness and Alterity: A Phenomenological Investigation*. Evanston, IL: Northwestern University Press.

Zahavi, D. (1999b). Michel Henry and the phenomenology of the invisible. *Continental Philosophy Review* 32(3): 223–240.

Zahavi, D. (2001). *Husserl and Transcendental Intersubjectivity*, trans. E. Behnke. Athens, OH: Ohio University Press.

Zahavi, D. (2003). *Husserl's Phenomenology*. Stanford, CA: Stanford University Press.

Zahavi, D. (2004). *Phenomenology and the project of naturalization. Phenomenology and the Cognitive Sciences* 3(4): 331–347.

Zahavi, D. (2005). *Subjectivity and Selfhood: Investigating the First-Person Perspective*. Cambridge, MA: MIT Press.

Zahavi, D. (2011). Empathy and direct social perception: A phenomenological proposal. *Review of Philosophy and Psychology* 2(3): 541–558.

Zahavi, D. (ed.) (2012). *The Oxford Handbook of Contemporary Phenomenology*. Oxford: Oxford University Press.

Zahavi, D. (2013). Naturalized phenomenology: A desideratum or a category mistake? *Royal Institute of Philosophy Supplements* 72: 23–42.

Zahavi, D. (2014). *Self and Other: Exploring Subjectivity, Empathy, and Shame*. Oxford: Oxford University Press.

Zahavi, D. (2017). *Husserl's Legacy: Phenomenology, Metaphysics, and Transcendental Philosophy*. Oxford: Oxford University Press.

Zahavi, D. (2019). Second-person engagement, self-alienation, and group-identification. *Topoi* 38: 251–260.

Zahavi, D. (2025). *Being We: Phenomenological Contributions to Social Ontology*. Oxford: Oxford University Press.

INDEX

Printed in the United States
by Baker & Taylor Publisher Services